# My Boss is Insane

## And Other Workplace Nightmares

Richard Lowe

The Writing King

**My Boss is Insane: And Other Workplace Nightmares**

Copyright © 2026 by Richard G Lowe

# Table of Contents

See books by Richard Lowe at

https://masterofworlds.com


Get free publishing insights and industry updates at

https://thewritingking.substack.com


For ghostwriting and book coaching services see

https://thewritingking.com

# Legal Disclaimer

This book is intended for informational and educational purposes only. The author is not a lawyer, licensed therapist, or employment counselor. The advice and strategies contained herein are based on the author's personal experiences and observations over thirty-three years in corporate environments.

The information in this book should not be considered legal advice, and readers should consult with qualified employment attorneys regarding their specific situations, especially those involving discrimination, harassment, or potential legal action. Employment laws vary significantly by state, country, and jurisdiction.

While the author has made every effort to provide accurate and helpful information, workplace situations are complex and individual circumstances vary greatly. Readers are responsible for their own career decisions and should consider their personal financial and professional situations before acting on any advice in this book.

The stories contained in this book are based on real experiences, though names and identifying details have been changed to protect privacy. Any resemblance to specific people or companies is coincidental.

Neither the author nor publisher assumes any liability for actions taken by readers based on information contained in this book. If you are experiencing workplace harassment, discrimination, or safety concerns, please consult with appropriate professionals including legal counsel, mental health providers, or law enforcement as warranted.

# Preface

This book exists because too many people are suffering in silence.

Every week, I meet someone who tells me about their terrible boss. The micromanager who tracks bathroom breaks. The liar who steals commissions. The racist who makes "jokes" in meetings. The psychotic executive who screams at employees until they cry. The sexual predator who uses power to hunt subordinates.

These stories are depressingly similar to the ones I lived through during my thirty-three years in corporate America. The names and companies change, but the patterns of dysfunction remain constant. Bad managers get promoted, good employees get driven away, and the cycle continues.

What frustrates me most is how isolated these victims feel. They think they're the only ones dealing with impossible bosses. They blame themselves for not being able to "handle" abuse that would break anyone. They stay trapped in toxic situations because they don't realize how common these problems are or that there are ways to fight back.

I wrote this book to break that isolation. Every story in here actually happened (the names and circumstances have been changed). Every toxic behavior I describe exists in workplaces across America. If you're dealing with a boss who makes your life miserable, you're not alone, you're not crazy, and you're not powerless.

I learned that you don't have to accept abuse just because someone has authority over you. I learned that documentation is your best protection against liars and manipulators. I learned that financial independence gives you the power to walk away from toxic situations. Most importantly, I learned that there are good managers out there, and you don't have to settle for the disasters.

The workplace doesn't have to be a source of trauma and stress. You deserve better than what too many of these managers offer. This book will show you how to recognize the warning signs, protect yourself from the worst behaviors, and build the skills and resources that give you real choices about where and how you work.

Your career is too important to leave in the hands of toxic managers. Your mental health is too valuable to sacrifice for any paycheck. Take back control of your professional life.

You have more power than you think.

# Introduction

Most of us have a person called the boss, a manager or supervisor who has authority over our actions in the workplace. In an ideal situation, the boss has the power to maintain an environment that is creative and supportive.

They work with us to set goals that align with company objectives. Once those are defined, a good manager gets out of the way, delegates appropriate authority and responsibility, and lets us do our jobs. Discipline is mild; any issues with performance are handled immediately, making the annual review process very simple.

Unfortunately, the ideal boss is a rarity in today's workplace.

Many times, supervisors and managers get promoted with little, if any, training. These people often mean well, but since they do not have the knowledge or background to understand working with teams, they tend to make many errors and often alienate their people.

Business courses in college teach theoretical concepts that may not translate well into a real-life workplace. These well-schooled managers enter the workplace believing they know exactly what they are doing, and they often start with an air of arrogance and heavy-handedness that alienates their staff.

Some managers have personalities that make them a terror in the workplace. A racist or sexist boss can create a very hostile working environment for their subordinates. A boss who is retiring can become very cautious since they don't want to rock the boat and put their pension in jeopardy. Those who micromanage or are unethical create many problems with their staff. And, of course, the psychotic or hostile manager creates far more problems than they solve.

The boss can be a real problem for subordinates because they're in a position of power over them, regardless of whether they're competent. In a disagreement, their word is favored over those they manage. Often, the boss is more trusted than the people who work for them.

The higher up the organizational chart, the more of a problem this becomes. An incompetent, harassing, or hostile boss is a headache at any level, but at Vice-President or higher can set a tone for the entire corporation. If the CEO encourages ethics and competence, then those below will tend to be ethical and competent. If the CEO is hostile, angry, or fearful, then the managers underneath will take on the same characteristics. Lack of ethics at the top, by the way, is how a massive company like Enron could do so much harm.

For those who like a calm, stable, and fulfilling job, these managers and so-called leaders make the entire organization a very unpleasant place to work.

In this book, I've included examples of different bosses I've encountered over thirty-three years of working or consulting for companies, from the quietly racist manager to the psychotic executive who needed armed guards to be fired. The idea is to present scenarios from my own experience and suggest some things that you can do to help yourself in that situation. Please note that I've changed names and some details to protect people's privacy, but every story actually happened.

A hostile environment supported by the boss can make a person sick, depressed, anxious, and unmotivated. If you can't fix the situation by communicating with your boss and other people in the organization, you may have no choice but to move on to somewhere more pleasant.

You should always ensure that you can leave your job if necessary without undue hardship. (See Chapter 14 for detailed financial planning strategies.)

This isn't a book written by an expert or consultant. I'm not a psychologist, lawyer, or business school professor. I'm someone who survived thirty-three years in corporate America and learned some hard lessons along the way. Some of those lessons cost me jobs. Some cost me money. A few nearly cost me my sanity.

But I learned you don't have to tolerate abuse, harassment, or unethical behavior from anyone, regardless of their title. Your integrity is more important than any job. You can always find a new job.

# Chapter 1: What a Good Boss Actually Looks Like



I got lucky with my first boss. His name was Steve Davis, and he became my model for what competent management should look like. I didn't realize how fortunate I was until years later, after I'd worked for a parade of disasters who showed me just how rare good leadership actually is.

Steve was a technology executive who eventually became a Vice President at Disney, serving on their IT Leadership Board and Enterprise Architecture Board. But when I worked for him early in my career, he was still building his reputation as one of the most technically competent and organizationally savvy managers I've ever encountered.

What made Steve different wasn't any single dramatic gesture. It was the accumulation of dozens of small things that created an environment where people could actually do their jobs effectively.

First, Steve knew what he was talking about. This seems obvious, but you'd be amazed how many managers get promoted without understanding the technical aspects of what their teams do. Steve had deep expertise in both technology and business. When he made decisions, they were based on real knowledge, not guesswork or politics. If he didn't know something, he said so and found out. He never pretended to have expertise he lacked.

Second, he communicated clearly and consistently. When Steve gave you an assignment, you understood exactly what was expected, when it was due, and how success would be measured. There were no moving goalposts, no vague instructions that left you guessing what he really wanted. If priorities changed (and they sometimes did), he explained why and adjusted timelines accordingly. You never felt like you were being set up to fail.

Steve also understood delegation. Once he assigned you a project, he got out of your way and let you do the work. He didn't micromanage or constantly check over your shoulder. He was available if you needed guidance or resources, but he trusted his people to handle their responsibilities. This created an environment where you could actually focus on getting things done instead of managing your manager's anxiety.

When problems arose (and they always do), Steve addressed them immediately and directly. If you made a mistake, he'd discuss it with you privately, help you understand what went wrong, and figure out how to prevent it in the future. There was no public humiliation, no passive-aggressive punishment, no holding grudges. The focus was always on solving the problem and moving forward.

Steve also protected his team from organizational chaos. In every company, there are unreasonable demands, political fights, and resource constraints that create stress. Good managers shield their people from as much of this as possible. Steve would take the pressure from above us and translate it into manageable tasks for his team. When upper management demanded the impossible, Steve would push back or find creative solutions rather than just passing the stress down to us.

Steve treated people with respect. He listened when you had concerns or suggestions. He gave credit where it was due and took responsibility when things went wrong. He never threw his people under the bus to make himself look better. He understood that his success depended on his team's success, so he invested in helping people develop their skills and advance their careers.

I remember one particular situation where a project I was working on hit a major technical snag. The deadline was firm, the client was important, and I was genuinely stuck. I went to Steve expecting to get chewed out for not having anticipated the problem. Instead, he sat down with me, listened to the issue, asked good questions, and helped brainstorm solutions. Within an hour, we had a plan that got the project back on track. His response was: "These things happen. Let's fix it and document what we learned so we don't hit this again."

That's what competent management looks like.

Steve also understood the difference between being demanding and being unreasonable. He had high standards and expected people to meet them. But those standards were achievable by competent people with adequate resources. He didn't ask for miracles or expect people to work impossible hours to compensate for poor planning. When he did ask people to put in extra effort, it was for legitimate emergencies, not manufactured crises.


These aren't revolutionary concepts. They're basic management competencies that should be standard in any well-run organization. The tragedy is how rare they actually are.

Working for Steve taught me what good leadership looks like in practice. It set my expectations for what I should expect from future managers and what I should strive for when I eventually managed people myself. It also gave me a baseline for recognizing when management was failing, because I had experienced what success actually felt like.

The contrast becomes stark when you work for incompetent, unethical, or abusive managers. You realize that the calm productivity and mutual respect you experienced with good leadership wasn't just luck. It resulted from specific skills and behaviors that can be learned and practiced.

Most organizations don't invest in developing these skills in their managers. People get promoted based on technical expertise or political connections, not leadership ability. The result is workplaces filled with managers who mean well but don't know how to manage, or worse, managers who create toxic environments through their own dysfunction.

Steve showed me it doesn't have to be that way. Good management is possible, and when you experience it, you realize how much better work can be when it's done right.

The stories in the rest of this book are about what happens when it goes wrong. But before I describe the disasters, I wanted you to know what the alternative looks like. Because once you've experienced competent leadership, you'll never again accept the excuse that bad management is just "how things are."

It isn't. It's a choice.

And, truly, over the years I missed Steve and his excellent management style. He was a gem among unpolished stones.


I had one other boss, years later, who demonstrated similar competence, though with a completely different style. John Shields had been CEO at major companies like Macy's and Trader Joe's. When he came to our company as the new CEO, I was nervous. He had a reputation for being tough, direct, maybe even intimidating.

A few days after he started, I needed to spend $70,000 on a new computer system. This was a significant expense, and I wasn't sure how the new CEO would react. I approached him nervously and explained that we needed the system to improve our service capabilities, but I didn't know if it would be funded.

In his gruff manner, he looked at me and said, "You worry about the technology, I'll worry about funding. You say it will improve service? Do it."

That was John's style. Quick, to the point, and he delegated authority. Where Steve was collaborative and nurturing, John was decisive and direct. But both approaches worked because they were based on the same foundation: competence, clear communication, and trust in their people.

John understood that his job was to remove obstacles, not create them. He made decisions quickly so his team could move forward. He didn't second-guess the expertise he'd hired or bog people down with endless approvals for things that clearly needed to be done.

Both Steve and John showed me that good leadership comes in different styles, but it always includes certain core elements: knowledge of the business, clear expectations, appropriate delegation, and respect for the people doing the work.

# Chapter 2: The Boss Is Racist

---

*"The way to stop discrimination on the basis of race is to stop discriminating on the basis of race." — John Roberts*

---

After working for competent managers like Steve Davis and John Shields, I thought I understood how workplace hierarchies functioned. You did good work, your boss recognized it, and you advanced based on merit. I was naive enough to believe the system was fundamentally fair.

That illusion shattered when I encountered my first openly racist boss.

Sally was a mid-level manager who had worked hard on performance reviews that year, spending hours evaluating each of her six subordinates. One of her team members was a black man named Roscoe who had done exceptional work throughout the year. He was always willing to come into the office, always helpful, and pitched in whenever needed.

Sally turned in her reviews to her boss with suggested raises for each person. The range was from 1% to 4%, and since she felt Roscoe had done such outstanding work, she gave him the highest raise at 4%. Everyone else got between 2% and 3.5%.

In the past, her boss had never made changes to her recommendations and always allowed each team member to receive the raise she suggested.

This year was different.

When the reviews came back, the boss had changed Roscoe's raise to 2% and modified David's (a white employee) to 4%. There was no explanation. Sally's numbers were simply crossed out and replaced with new values.

"Boss," she said when she saw the changes, "what's up with these modifications?"

"David is an outstanding performer," he replied, "and that needs to be recognized."

"I can understand that," she said, "but why have you lowered Roscoe's raise?"

"You know there's only a certain amount of money, and if I raise one I have to lower another."

Sally paused, thinking. "You know, Roscoe worked hard this year, and I'd like to keep that 4% raise for him."

The boss and Sally went back and forth for several minutes, and the conversation became more heated.

"Hey," he finally yelled, obviously getting angry, "I'm the boss, and he's just a damn n…"

He trailed off as he realized what he was about to say.

Sally stood there for a moment, mouth open, not quite believing what she had just heard. Of course, she suspected what was happening, but she never expected him to nearly say it out loud.

"Boss," she said, taking a moment to regain her composure, "we'll keep the raises I recommended."

"Like hell you will," he said.

"Well, sure," Sally replied calmly. "Why don't we continue this conversation in human resources? How about we show them this piece of paper with your changes?"

The boss glared at her, turned around, and left. Sally put in the raise amounts as she had originally recommended, ignoring his changes, and that's what everyone received.

Sally expected her manager to make her life difficult after that confrontation. The strange thing was, the subject never came up again. Even better, she never detected a hint of racism from him again.

Looking back, Sally realized she had learned something important about standing up to workplace discrimination. When she challenged the racist behavior directly and made it clear there would be consequences (involving HR and creating a paper trail), the boss backed down completely.

I saw another situation where the discrimination was more subtle but equally damaging.

Hassan was working on a project ahead of schedule with a happy customer when his subordinate Daniela approached him.

"Why haven't you promoted me?" she asked directly.

"I think you're doing fine in the position you're at," Hassan replied.

"You're evading the question. Give me a straight answer. You promoted several people over me. What's wrong with my performance?"

Hassan looked down at his desk, avoiding her eyes.

"I was right," Daniela said. "What's going on?"

"Nothing at all, Daniela. Everything is completely fine."

"Everything's not fine. You passed me over for promotion three times now. I want to know why."

"I don't have anything else to tell you."

"Is it because I'm Israeli?" Daniela asked boldly.

Hassan was silent, continuing to focus on the papers in front of him.

"That is why!" Daniela exclaimed.

"As I said, I have nothing else to say."

"I'm heading over to human resources," Daniela said. "We'll see what they have to say about this."

"You do what you have to do," Hassan replied.

Daniela went to HR but didn't get much support. Without concrete documentation, HR said there was nothing they could do. (See Chapter 11 for why HR departments typically respond this way.)

Frustrated, Daniela eventually found a job somewhere else.


These two stories show the different faces of workplace racism. Sometimes it's blatant, like Sally's boss nearly using a racial slur. Sometimes it's subtle, like Hassan's pattern of passing over qualified employees based on their ethnicity or nationality.

Sally's situation worked out because she had concrete evidence (the boss's written changes to the performance reviews) and she was willing to confront the behavior directly. When she threatened to involve HR and create a paper trail, the racist boss backed down immediately.

Daniela's case went nowhere because she had no documentation, just a pattern she could observe but not prove. Hassan never said anything overtly discriminatory. He never put his prejudice in writing. He just consistently passed over a qualified employee for advancement.

The difference in outcomes shows why documentation matters so much. Sally had physical proof of discriminatory action. Daniela had suspicions and observations, but no evidence that would hold up in an HR investigation or legal proceeding.


Racism in the workplace takes many forms, from overt slurs to subtle patterns of discrimination. The key is recognizing it, documenting it, and confronting it when possible. You can't always change racist people, but you can sometimes stop racist behavior by making the consequences unacceptable. (Note: Discrimination laws vary by jurisdiction and situation — consult with an employment attorney for advice specific to your circumstances.)

The most striking thing about Sally's story was how quickly the racist behavior stopped once it was challenged. Many workplace racists are cowards who will only discriminate when they think they can get away with it. When faced with someone willing to fight back, they retreat.

But as Daniela's experience shows, not all discrimination is so easily defeated. Sometimes the racist behavior is careful, subtle, and hard to prove. In those cases, the victim often has little choice but to leave for a better environment.

Neither outcome is acceptable. Racism has no place in any workplace, and employees shouldn't have to choose between tolerating discrimination and finding new jobs. But until organizations get serious about rooting out discriminatory managers, these will continue to be the only options for many people.

The cost of staying silent is too high, not just for the immediate victims, but for everyone who has to work in that toxic environment.

Workplace racism creates ripple effects that damage entire organizations. When discriminatory managers face no consequences, other employees learn that bias is acceptable. Talented people from diverse backgrounds avoid companies with reputations for discrimination, limiting the talent pool and stunting innovation. Customers and clients may also distance themselves from organizations known for racist practices.

The economic cost is substantial too. Companies face lawsuits, settlements, and regulatory penalties. They lose productivity when good employees leave and when remaining staff operates under stress and fear. The damage to company culture can take years to repair, long after the racist manager is finally removed.

This is why documentation and direct confrontation matter so much. Every time someone like Sally stands up to discriminatory behavior, they're not just protecting one employee — they're protecting the integrity of the entire workplace.

# Chapter 3: The Boss Is Harassing Religion



Religious harassment in the workplace is often more subtle than racial discrimination, but it can be just as damaging. I learned this firsthand when I encountered a boss who couldn't tolerate employees whose faith differed from his own narrow worldview.

Duane was interviewing for a personal assistant position at the request of his boss, Gary. It was a new company expanding rapidly, and Gary was finding himself overworked. He needed someone to help him organize, make phone calls, set up meetings, and handle the books.

The candidate, Lucy, had talked to Duane about the position, and they agreed to meet at Baker's Square for the interview. The company was too young to have an office, so a lot of work got done in local restaurants.

Originally, Gary was supposed to conduct the interview, but he was running late and called asking Duane to handle it instead.

"So you have several years' experience as an office manager?" Duane asked.

"Yes," Lucy replied. "I was the office manager for a company called Neco-ware. I also went to school and learned bookkeeping."

The interview proceeded well for thirty minutes, and Duane established that Lucy had the necessary qualifications for the job.

Gary still hadn't arrived by the time they finished, leaving Duane and Lucy a few minutes to talk and get to know each other.

"How long have you lived in Connecticut?" Lucy asked.

"I moved here about a year ago," Duane replied. "I was tired of Texas; it's always hot and dry."

"That it is," Lucy said, laughing. "Do you like Connecticut so far?"

"I do," Duane replied. "I still haven't met a lot of people, though."

"Why don't you look for people in your church?" Lucy asked.

"I haven't found any pagan groups yet," Duane replied.

"You're pagan?" Lucy asked.

"Oh, yes," Duane said. "Specifically, Wiccan."

Lucy had never heard of that religion before, so she spent the next fifteen minutes asking questions. She was genuinely interested to learn this was a very peaceful religion and seemed happy with what she heard.

Gary finally arrived, about an hour late, and did his part of the interview. Duane did some shopping at the local store to kill time, then returned so he and Gary could discuss how the interview went. It was a tiny company, brand new, so Gary wanted to make sure they got the right person for the job.

"You told her you're pagan," Gary said, irritation evident in his voice.

"Of course," Duane replied. "I am pagan."

"I know that," Gary replied. "Don't tell clients or employees about your religion."

"You just told me not to talk about my religion?" Duane said, astounded at Gary's outburst.

"Yeah," Gary replied. "I don't care what religion you follow, but while you're working for me, don't talk about it here."

Duane looked at Gary and wondered for a moment if he was the subject of some sick joke. He peered into Gary's face and could see that he was indeed serious.

"I'm glad you told me that," Duane said. "And you know something, prejudices are disgusting, and I won't work for a person like you. I practice the Wiccan religion, and I'm proud of it."

"What are you telling me?" Gary asked.

"I quit," Duane replied.

"Let's talk about this," Gary said, his voice becoming much smoother.

"No," Duane replied. "There's nothing to say. You have a great day."

Duane got up and left the restaurant immediately. He was amazed at how good it felt to be in the position in life where he didn't have to take that kind of abuse from anyone.

What strikes me about this story is how quickly religious prejudice revealed itself. Gary didn't object to Duane's work performance, his qualifications, or his professional conduct. The moment he learned about Duane's religious beliefs, he demanded that Duane hide a fundamental part of his identity.

This is religious harassment in its most basic form: the demand that employees suppress their faith to make their boss comfortable. Gary tried to frame it as a business decision ("don't talk about it here"), but his real message was clear: your religion is unacceptable to me.

Duane's response was perfect. He recognized the prejudice immediately, called it out directly, and refused to work in that environment. He was fortunate to be in a financial position where he could walk away, but not everyone has that luxury.

Religious harassment takes many forms in the workplace: direct hostility toward specific faiths, jokes and comments that demean particular religious groups, scheduling conflicts that force employees to choose between their job and their religious observances, dress codes that prohibit religious clothing or symbols, managers who push their own beliefs on subordinates, and exclusion from meetings or opportunities based on religious differences.

What Gary did to Duane was both illegal and morally wrong. Employees have the right to discuss their religious beliefs in casual workplace conversations, just as they might discuss their weekend plans or family activities. Demanding that someone hide their faith is discrimination.

Religious harassment often starts small and escalates if not challenged. It might begin with jokes about someone's religious practices, then progress to exclusion from workplace social events, and eventually affect performance reviews and advancement opportunities.

I've seen managers who assumed everyone shared their Christian faith and made comments that excluded employees of other religions. I've watched supervisors roll their eyes when Jewish employees needed to leave early for religious holidays, even though company policy clearly provided for such accommodations.

The worst form of religious harassment is creating an environment where employees feel they must hide their faith to fit in or advance. When managers make it clear through words and actions that certain religious beliefs are unwelcome, employees get the message and start self-censoring.

This creates a toxic workplace where diversity of thought and belief is suppressed in favor of conformity to whatever religious viewpoint the boss finds acceptable.

Gary's demand that Duane keep his religion secret revealed a profound misunderstanding of both the law and basic human dignity. Employers don't get to pick and choose which religious beliefs are acceptable in their workplace, any more than they get to discriminate based on race or gender.

The fact that Gary backed down and tried to negotiate when Duane quit shows that many religious bigots are ultimately cowards who back off when confronted directly. But the damage was already done. Gary had revealed his true character, and Duane was smart enough to recognize that this wasn't someone he could work for successfully.

If you encounter religious harassment, start by documenting everything. Keep records of harassing comments, denied accommodations, and any patterns of discriminatory treatment.

Know your rights. The law requires employers to accommodate religious practices unless doing so creates undue hardship. You have the right to practice your religion and discuss it in appropriate workplace contexts — demanding that someone hide their faith is discrimination, not a business decision. (Employment law is complex and varies by state — consult an attorney for guidance on your specific situation.)

Duane's decision to walk away was the right choice for his situation, but not everyone can afford to quit immediately when faced with religious harassment. For those who need to keep their jobs while fighting discrimination, building a solid case with documentation and witnesses is crucial.

Religious harassment is particularly damaging because it attacks something fundamental to many people's identity. When a boss tells you to hide your faith, they're essentially telling you to hide who you are. That's not just illegal; it's dehumanizing.

Everyone deserves to work in an environment where their fundamental beliefs are respected, even if not shared by their colleagues or supervisors. Religious harassment has no place in any professional setting, and employees have both the right and the responsibility to confront it when it occurs.

# Chapter 4: The Boss Is a Liar

*"Before lying to one who trusts you remember one of the difficult things to do is to build trust after it has been broken."*
— *Anurag Prakash Ray*

Nothing destroys workplace morale faster than a boss who lies. Not the little white lies that everyone tells ("I'll get back to you on that"), but the deliberate deceptions that cost employees money, opportunities, and faith in their leadership. I learned this lesson the hard way when I worked for managers who treated promises like disposable tools to extract more work from their teams.

The owner of a startup company, a man named Stan, was an incredibly nice guy who could talk with the best of them. Like many entrepreneurs, he had grand visions and the gift of making others believe in them. The company was only a few years old and sold consulting services to help businesses with their personal computers.

As with many startups, there was a lot of work and not enough money or resources to do it all. Stan had some great ideas, and the company went off in several directions at the same time. It soon became apparent that he would need to hire a couple of programmers and perhaps a manager to keep things moving.

At that point, he received a phone call from José, who was looking for a job. José had a job, but the company he was with was showing signs of distress. Thirty percent of the workforce had been laid off, and rumor had it that the owners used their personal credit cards to cover some of the paychecks.

Stan offered José a position at much less than José was worth on the open market.

"Don't worry," Stan said. "Come on board, and when this company takes off, there'll be more in it for you."

That sounded good to José. He was feeling stuck in his standard 9-to-5 job and felt like it was time to get a taste of something bigger, perhaps even stock options down the road.

Within the first couple of months, José was making an impact on the business. He was managing four people and juggling about a dozen projects at the same time. Business was booming, and everything was going well.

Since it was a consulting business, there was always the need for more jobs coming in.

"Any business you bring in," Stan told José, "you get a 10% commission."

"That sounds great, boss," José said.

José added the responsibility of finding new work to his daily activities, even though it wasn't part of his job description. The promise of the commission, and perhaps even having a piece of the company down the road, was enticing.

"They signed the contract," José announced to Stan months later.

"Remind me how much it was again?" Stan said.

"It's an $850,000 project," José answered. "The biggest we've ever landed."

"That's great," Stan said. "Excellent job, thank you."

José waited a few days, expecting Stan to mention the commission, but nothing happened. Finally, after agonizing over how to bring up the subject, he decided he needed to talk to Stan.

"I thought you said I get a 10% commission if I brought in new business," José said.

"Oh," Stan said. "You misunderstood."

"How so?" José asked.

"I meant you get 10% if you bring in the new business on your own time. But since you did it on company time, you got paid for it already as part of your salary."

José sat in the chair, dumbfounded, not knowing what to say. He'd been putting in eighty-hour weeks for over a year, pouring his entire life into this small consulting company.

"But boss..." José began.

"That's all there is to it," Stan said. "There's nothing more to say."

José left that day very upset. After some thought, he decided not to quit, even though he felt like moving on. Instead, from that day forward, he worked forty-hour weeks and never reached out to bring in new business again.

I've seen this scenario replay many times throughout my career, and I've experienced that frustration myself. I'm a technical person and a manager, not a salesperson. Even so, on several occasions, I've been promised commissions for getting new business. However, when push came to shove, those commissions never materialized.

In every case, the boss, generally the owner of the company, claimed that because the sale was made on company time or during company events, no commission was to be paid.

The result was always the same: complete demoralization. Hours dropped to the minimum required, creativity disappeared, and any sense of responsibility went out the window.

This doesn't just apply to promised commissions. Companies often make vague promises of future rewards, such as stock options or "a piece of the company" in return for putting in extra hours without immediate compensation.

Without fail, every time a boss has made this kind of promise to me personally (and this has happened many times), they have failed to fulfill their end of the bargain. Not once has an owner or boss ever delivered on these nebulous future rewards. Not to me, not to my peers, and not to anyone else in my entire network.

The psychology behind these lies is simple: the boss needs extra work done but doesn't want to pay for it immediately. So they dangle future rewards that cost nothing to promise but everything to deliver. When the work is done and the crisis has passed, suddenly those promises become "misunderstandings" or get forgotten entirely.

Stan's lie to José was particularly cruel because it was premeditated. He didn't make an impulsive promise in a moment of desperation. He deliberately created a compensation structure that he never intended to honor. When José delivered an $850,000 contract, Stan had his excuse ready: it was done on company time.

This wasn't a misunderstanding. It was theft.

The most damaging thing about working for pathological liars isn't just the money you lose. It's the way it changes your relationship with work itself. When you can't trust your boss's promises, you stop going the extra mile. You stop believing in the company's mission. You stop caring about anything beyond your immediate job requirements.

José's response was completely rational. Why bring in new business if you won't be compensated for it? Why work eighty-hour weeks if extra effort isn't valued? Why invest emotionally in a company led by someone who lies to your face?

Lying bosses create exactly the kind of disengaged workforce they claim to despise. They complain that employees "just punch the clock" and don't show initiative, never recognizing that their own dishonesty destroyed whatever motivation their people once had.


José's experience taught me several hard lessons about protecting yourself from dishonest managers. The most important is getting everything in writing. When a boss promises a commission, bonus, or any future reward, you need to insist on written documentation. Verbal promises become worthless the moment a dishonest manager decides to rewrite history, as Stan did when he claimed José had "misunderstood" their agreement about the 10% commission.

I also learned never to work for free based on vague future promises. If extra work is genuinely needed, the time to negotiate fair compensation is upfront, not after you've already delivered results. Those assurances about "more money later" or "equity down the road" are tools that dishonest managers use to extract free labor, and they almost never materialize into actual compensation.

Perhaps most importantly, once you catch a boss in a deliberate lie about compensation, the working relationship is essentially over. They will lie again because that's who they are, and you'll never be able to trust anything they say. This isn't about you personally — pathological liars like Stan don't target specific people. They lie to everyone about everything because it's a fundamental character flaw, not a reflection of your worth or performance.

The only rational response is to start planning your exit immediately, because staying means accepting that your boss considers you gullible enough to work for promises they never intend to keep.

For detailed strategies on documenting toxic boss behavior, see Chapter 12.


The saddest part of José's story is that he stayed at the company after being lied to. He reduced his effort and stopped bringing in new business, but he remained employed by someone who had stolen from him. This allowed Stan to continue his pattern with other employees.

When bosses face no consequences for lying, they keep lying. The only way to stop dishonest managers is to make their lies expensive. This means leaving when you catch them in deliberate deception, taking your skills and knowledge with you.

Some lies are worse than others. Forgetting about a casual conversation is different from deliberately creating false expectations about compensation. Missing a deadline is different from promising rewards you never intend to deliver.

Pathological lying by managers destroys trust, kills motivation, and creates toxic work environments where everyone operates from a position of suspicion and self-protection.

Your integrity is more valuable than any job. Don't compromise it by continuing to work for people who have no integrity themselves.

# Chapter 5: The Boss Is Retiring

*"There are some who start their retirement long before they stop working." — Robert Half*

Working for a boss who won't make decisions is almost worse than working for one who makes bad ones. At least with bad decisions, you know where you stand and can plan accordingly. With an absentee manager who has mentally checked out, you're left in limbo, unable to move forward on anything significant.

I experienced this frustration with a boss who had announced his retirement and gave twelve months' notice. From the day he made that announcement, he became a ghost in his own office.

"Boss," I said one morning, "have you looked at my proposal?"

"Not yet," he replied. "Don't worry, I'll get to it this week."

"I don't mean to be rude," I said with a sigh, "but you've been telling me that for over a month now."

"Yeah, I know. I'm sorry, I really will get to it."

"I know you will," I said. "It's just that this is important. We need to get this equipment installed."

The proposal was for equipment that wasn't in the budget, and the amount was large enough that it needed to go up one level of the organization for approval. I had the authority to make routine purchases within defined limits, but there were several new projects, completely outside the budget, which required equipment and manpower that needed approval from above.

"I'll bring it to my boss today," he replied quietly. I could see that he was not thrilled with the prospect.

To my surprise, he actually carried through with his promise and brought it to his boss, who promptly shot it down. We eventually did purchase the equipment, but only after the old machines failed completely and we had no choice.

This became the pattern. Since announcing his retirement, nothing got approved, there was little discussion of anything substantive, and decisions got postponed until the last possible second. It was a frustrating time, as I was unable to perform many of the duties of my position.

My peers and I had the authority to make routine purchases needed to run our operations. We had some freedom to buy equipment and hire consultants, within defined limits. But there were several new projects that required resources beyond our individual budgets, and all of those projects stalled for lack of resources.

As his retirement day approached, I kept glancing at the stack of proposals and orders on my desk. All of them were important, all had been written and justified, but none had been approved. It was becoming evident that I would need to get those approvals from the new boss, and there was no way to predict if he would approve them or not.

One month before leaving, the retiring boss walked over to my desk, spotted the stack of proposals and orders, and signed every one of them. Perhaps it was close enough to retirement that he felt he had nothing to lose.

Finally! I thought. It's such a relief to be allowed to do my job.

The psychology of the retiring boss is understandable but destructive. He didn't want to rock the boat or make any controversial decisions that might complicate his final months. Every decision carried the risk of conflict, pushback, or having to defend a position. It was easier to just avoid making decisions altogether.

But this avoidance paralyzed everyone who worked for him. Projects couldn't move forward. Equipment couldn't be purchased. New hires couldn't be approved. The entire department was stuck in neutral while he ran out the clock.

What made this particularly frustrating was that these weren't controversial or risky decisions. They were routine business needs that any competent manager should have been able to approve or reject quickly. The equipment we needed was standard stuff. The projects were well within normal business parameters.

His reluctance to make decisions wasn't protecting the company from bad choices. It was preventing good work from getting done.

If you find yourself working for a boss who has checked out:

Keep communicating with your manager, but don't expect much. Document your requests so there's a paper trail showing you tried to get proper approvals. Try to negotiate expanded decision-making authority — absentee bosses often delegate more than usual because it's easier than making decisions themselves. Build relationships with your boss's peers or superiors so you have alternative paths when critical issues arise. Maintain your own work quality regardless of your boss's disengagement, and be prepared for a flood of signatures near the end — many checked-out managers will eventually clear their desk before leaving.

For comprehensive exit planning strategies when the situation becomes untenable, see Chapter 14.

The most damaging aspect of working for a retiring boss isn't the delayed decisions, though that's certainly frustrating. It's the message it sends to the team that their work doesn't matter enough to warrant attention from leadership.

When a manager stops engaging with the daily needs of the business, it creates a sense of abandonment among the staff.

People start to wonder if their projects are worthwhile, if their requests are reasonable, or if they're doing something wrong.

This erosion of confidence can last long after the retiring manager is gone. The new boss inherits a team that has learned to expect inaction and delay from leadership.

The retiring boss phenomenon isn't limited to people who are actually retiring. I've seen the same behavior from managers who have been passed over for promotion, are unhappy with organizational changes, or are simply burned out and disengaged.

The common thread is a manager who has mentally moved on from the job while still physically occupying the position. They're collecting a paycheck but not doing the work, and their teams suffer the consequences.

The key is not to let your boss's disengagement affect your own performance. Continue doing your job at a high level, document your efforts to get necessary approvals, and build relationships that will help you succeed regardless of your immediate supervisor's limitations.

My retiring boss finally signed all those proposals in his last month, but by then we had lost nearly a year of progress on important projects. Some of that lost time was recoverable, but some opportunities were simply gone.

The experience taught me that when I became a manager, I needed to maintain engagement right up until my last day. Your team depends on you to do the job you're paid to do, regardless of your personal transition plans.

Leadership is a responsibility, not just a role, and that responsibility doesn't diminish just because you're planning to leave.

I encountered this same pattern with a different manager who had been passed over for a promotion she expected. Like my retiring boss, she mentally checked out while still collecting her paycheck. Projects stalled, decisions were avoided, and her team felt abandoned. The only difference was that her disengagement had no end date — she just drifted through her remaining years until actual retirement.

# Chapter 6: The Boss Is Unethical

---

*"Integrity is not a conditional word. It doesn't blow in the wind or change with the weather. It is your inner image of yourself, and if you look in there and see a man who won't cheat, then you know he never will." — John D. MacDonald*

---

What do you do when your boss asks you to be a party to what you feel is unethical behavior? Not an illegal act or a flagrant ethical violation, just something that violates your sense of right and wrong.

"I'll put together a proposal justifying purchasing that new equipment," Roger told his boss.

"No, that's okay," he replied.

"I don't need a proposal?" Roger replied. He was puzzled by the response because this was a major purchase exceeding a hundred thousand dollars. Why wouldn't he need to write a proposal, if only to formally document the reasons behind the requirement?

"I don't want this on the radar," the boss said, carefully avoiding his eyes.

"Oh, why not?"

"We don't have it in the budget," he replied.

"Oh, okay," Roger replied. "But we have to get this equipment..."

He started to explain the reasons.

"Oh, I know that," the boss interrupted. "Go ahead and make the purchase. Just bury it in the..." he picked up a spreadsheet from his desk, "...Nexus project budget."

"I can't do that, boss," Roger said. "It wouldn't be ethical. If it's not..."

"Okay," his boss replied, interrupting again, "well when you are ready, give me the PO, I'll sign it, and make sure the invoice comes to me. I'll take care of it." Roger could see that he was annoyed.

Roger left his desk confused and unhappy. Ethics is important, and this appeared to be a breach of good, honest behavior. Roger's opinion was that they should acknowledge that this equipment was missed during budgeting and make the purchase, or not, without playing games with the books.

Roger tried going to HR, but as often happens, they dismissed his ethical concerns and sided with the manager. (See Chapter 11 for a detailed analysis of how HR actually operates.)

This story illustrates one of the most insidious problems in corporate America: the normalization of unethical behavior through small compromises. Roger's boss wasn't asking him to embezzle money or commit fraud. He was just asking him to move an expense from one budget line to another to avoid awkward questions about overspending.

But that's how ethical erosion works. It starts with small violations that seem reasonable given the circumstances. "Everyone does it." "It's not hurting anyone." "We need to get the job done." "You know how it is around here."

Roger's instincts were correct. What his boss was asking was unethical. It was deliberately misrepresenting the true cost of projects to hide budget overruns. It was creating false financial records that would mislead anyone trying to understand the real economics of their operations.

More importantly, it was asking Roger to participate in the deception, making him complicit in behavior he knew was wrong.

The HR response was equally troubling. Rather than supporting an employee who was trying to maintain ethical standards, she dismissed his concerns and essentially told him to go along with whatever his boss wanted. This sends a clear message about the organization's real priorities: getting things done matters more than how you get them done.

I've encountered similar situations throughout my career. Bosses who wanted me to classify personal expenses as business costs. Managers who asked me to inflate time estimates to build padding into project budgets. Executives who wanted me to present misleading data to make their departments look more successful.

None of these requests involved major crimes or obvious fraud. They were all small ethical compromises that individually seemed minor but collectively created a culture where corners were routinely cut and rules were regularly bent.

The pressure to go along with unethical requests is enormous. Your boss has power over your performance reviews, your advancement opportunities, and ultimately your job security. Saying no to unethical requests can label you as "difficult," "not a team player," or "not understanding how business really works."

But the cost of going along is higher than the cost of refusing. Once you compromise your ethics for your boss, you've established that your principles have a price. The next request will be a little worse, and the one after that worse still, until you're doing things you never thought you'd do.

When facing unethical requests, start by separating the behavior from the attitude. You can't control what your boss thinks, but you can refuse to participate in actions you believe are wrong. Take some time before reacting — make sure you're not overreacting to something minor, but don't talk yourself out of a legitimate concern either.

In terms of concrete steps: first, give your boss a chance to reconsider by discussing the ethical implications directly — sometimes they haven't fully thought through what they're asking. Document everything, keeping records of the requests and your responses. If it rises to that level, consider reporting up the chain or to HR, though as Roger's story shows, don't expect much from HR. Be prepared to refuse participation in unethical activities even if it costs you politically. And make sure your finances are solid enough that you can leave if the compromises become intolerable.

Roger's situation was particularly frustrating because the ethical violation was unnecessary. The company needed the equipment, they had the money to buy it (since the boss was willing to approve the purchase), and there was probably a legitimate way to handle the budget issue. But rather than dealing with the paperwork and explanations required to do it properly, the boss chose to hide the expense in another project's budget.

This kind of casual dishonesty is corrosive to organizations. It creates parallel sets of books where the official records don't match reality. It makes it impossible for senior management to understand the true costs and profitability of different activities. It establishes a culture where deception is acceptable as long as it's convenient.

Unethical behavior affects everyone in the organization. When corners are cut and rules are bent regularly, employees learn that policies are suggestions rather than requirements. Quality suffers because shortcuts become routine. Customer trust erodes when they discover that the company doesn't operate with integrity.

Ethics starts at the top of a company. If upper management tolerates unethical behavior, employees quickly figure that out and adjust their own behavior accordingly. If senior leaders demand integrity and enforce ethical standards, that message travels down through the organization.

Roger was right to push back against his boss's request, even though he didn't get support from HR. He was also right to feel uncomfortable about the situation. His ethical instincts were functioning properly, telling him that something was wrong even if he couldn't articulate exactly what the problem was.

The tragedy is that Roger was essentially alone in his concern. His boss saw the request as routine business necessity. HR saw it as a minor accommodation to get work done. No one else in the organization seemed to think there was anything wrong with burying expenses in unrelated project budgets.

This isolation is one of the most challenging aspects of maintaining ethical standards in unethical organizations. When you're the only person who seems concerned about doing the right thing, you start to question whether you're being unreasonable or overly rigid.

You're not. Ethics matter, even for "small" violations that "everyone does." Your integrity is more valuable than your job, and compromising it for temporary career advantage is never worth the long-term cost to your character and self-respect.

Find organizations and managers who share your ethical standards. They exist. Don't settle for working in environments where doing the right thing is seen as a problem rather than a principle.

# Chapter 7: The Boss Is Micromanaging



"Have you found a solution yet?" the boss, Jose, asked while standing over Jim's shoulder. This was the fifth time he'd asked the same question in the last two hours, and it was getting annoying.

"No, boss," Jim replied, keeping his attention focused on the screen in front of him.

The merchandising application had been down for half the day, and no one had any clue as to what had happened. The first notification came from a call to the help desk at 2 am, and Jim and his team had been working the problem ever since. With only three hours of sleep under his belt, Jim was getting pretty grumpy, and the boss wasn't helping by staring over his shoulder.

"Well, when will you have it corrected?" Jose asked. Jim was always amazed at this question. Sure, he knew that everyone was on edge because the system was down. How could he know when the problem would be solved if he didn't even know what the problem was yet?

"Two hours, thirty-two minutes, and seventeen seconds from now," Jim replied with a straight face.

"Oh good, I'll let the...you're kidding me, right?"

"I'm sorry, boss. I've got no sleep, and I need to concentrate on this problem. Trust me, I'll let you know the second I have an answer for you."

"Okay," the boss replied, "You know it's important, right?"

Jim counted to twenty silently, attempting to control his temper. Of course, he knew it was important. He'd driven to the office at 2 am, woke up his entire team, and had everyone busy trying to find a solution.

"Yes, boss," Jim replied, keeping his voice even. "I do understand."

Sometimes micromanagement only occurs during emergencies, which is at least understandable. Everyone may be on edge and the boss could be catching pressure from above. However, when it occurs on a regular basis it becomes a serious problem.

I've worked for several micromanagers throughout my career, and the experience is always the same: constant interruptions, excessive oversight, and the feeling that your boss doesn't trust you to do the job you were hired to do.

The worst micromanager I ever encountered was a department head who required approval for every expense over $50. It didn't matter if you needed a $75 software manual or a $60 piece of hardware. Everything had to go through him personally, with written justification for why the expense was necessary.

He also insisted on reviewing every email before it was sent to anyone outside our department. Technical responses to customer questions, routine status updates to other teams, simple scheduling messages. Everything had to be approved. This created massive delays and made our entire department look incompetent to the rest of the organization.

But the worst part was the constant interruptions. He would walk by your desk every hour or so and ask what you were working on, how much progress you'd made, and when you expected to finish. If you were in the middle of debugging complex code or trying to solve a difficult technical problem, these interruptions were devastating to your concentration and productivity.

The irony is that micromanagers create exactly the problems they claim to be preventing. By constantly checking on people and requiring approval for routine decisions, they slow down work and introduce errors. Their lack of trust becomes a self-fulfilling prophecy as frustrated employees stop taking initiative and start doing only the minimum required.

Micromanagement stems from several sources. Some managers are simply insecure — they don't feel confident in their own abilities and try to control every detail to avoid any possibility of failure. Others were promoted without ever learning how to delegate, so they default to doing everything themselves. Sometimes the micromanagement is handed down: a boss who is being controlled from above often passes that anxiety straight to their team. And some people are simply control-addicted, uncomfortable unless they're involved in every decision. Finally, managers who have been burned by employee mistakes in the past sometimes overcompensate, eliminating any autonomy that might lead to future problems.

The damage caused by micromanagement extends far beyond just irritating employees. It destroys creativity and innovation because people stop suggesting improvements or trying new approaches. It prevents skill development because employees never get the chance to make decisions and learn from the consequences. It creates bottlenecks where everything waits for the manager's approval.

Most importantly, it drives away good employees. Competent people don't want to work in environments where they're treated like children who can't be trusted with basic responsibilities.

If you're dealing with a micromanager, have a conversation about how their management style affects your work. Focus on the impact on productivity and results, not on how it makes you feel. Many micromanagers don't realize how disruptive their behavior is.

Some practical steps that often help: proactively send regular status updates so your manager feels informed without needing to check constantly; ask explicitly for authority to handle routine decisions without approval, and get that in writing if possible; document your work and results so you have evidence of competence if your judgment is questioned; try to find out whether pressure from above is what's driving the behavior, since understanding the source can help you address the real problem; and if the interruptions are genuinely preventing you from working, have a direct conversation about appropriate times for check-ins and when you need uninterrupted focus.

The micromanager I mentioned earlier eventually left the company, and his replacement immediately eliminated most of the approval requirements and stopped the constant check-ins. Our department's productivity increased dramatically almost overnight. Projects that had been delayed for weeks because of approval bottlenecks were completed within days.

The difference was striking and made it clear how much damage the micromanagement had been doing. We hadn't realized how much time and energy we were spending on managing our manager's anxiety rather than doing our actual work.

Some managers confuse being demanding with being micromanaging. There's a big difference between having high standards and expecting quality results versus controlling every detail of how the work gets done. Good managers set clear expectations and then give people the freedom to meet those expectations in their own way.

Micromanagement is often a symptom of deeper organizational problems. Companies with cultures of fear and blame tend to produce managers who feel they need to control everything to protect themselves. Organizations that don't train their managers properly create supervisors who don't know how to delegate effectively.

The solution isn't to eliminate all oversight and accountability. Good management requires staying informed about what your team is doing and being available to provide guidance and support. The key is finding the right balance between staying informed and interfering with people's ability to do their jobs.

Trust is the foundation of effective management. If you hire competent people and give them clear expectations, most will perform well without constant supervision. If someone isn't performing well, address that specific problem rather than treating everyone like they can't be trusted.

# Chapter 8: The Boss Is Psychotic

---

*"When someone shows you who they are, believe them the first time." — Maya Angelou*

---

"You talked to Mary?" Jessica's boss, Alex, said to her as they passed in the halls.

"Sure," Jessica replied, "she wanted to know about…"

Alex interrupted her, "Don't do that again."

"Do what?" Jessica asked.

"Talk to anyone unless I am there," he replied.

Jessica nodded, indicating she understood.

Alex had built a wall around the department, claiming it was for their protection. No one was allowed to discuss anything with anyone outside of the group without his approval and, in most cases, his presence.

This rule made it difficult to get anything done.

Jessica walked back to her desk, which was up a flight of stairs, and worked on some reports for a while. An hour later, Alex stopped by and asked her to go for a walk with him "around the block." Jessica groaned internally. That usually meant he wanted to get away from the office so he could raise his voice and say something he didn't want others to hear.

They walked a few minutes until they were far from the office, and then Alex told Jessica, "I'm giving you a raise."

"Really?" she said.

"Yep," he replied. "A 35% increase in salary. I did some research, and my team is underpaid. So you are all getting raises to bring you in line with the rest of the industry."

Jessica pondered that for a moment. It was strange working for Alex. One day he was happy as can be, giving out huge raises to his managers. A few hours later, he would be chewing someone out for some minor offense, and the next day he was busily firing a consultant for no particular reason that Jessica could see.

Every expense, no matter how small, required his personal approval. It didn't matter if it was a book for $50 or a new computer for $100,000, the same level of authorization and justification was required. Sometimes he would approve without questions, other times he denied for no apparent reason.

The worst of it was the mood swings. He swung back and forth between manic and happy to angry and depressed throughout the day.

One day, he made it a point to show Jessica his new certificate. Alex looked proud as he pulled the framed piece of paper out from his drawer. He held it up, beaming as if he'd won a major award.

The certificate was from a psychiatrist who stated he was insane. Jessica remembered it had some psych terms like manic-depressive and bipolar or something like that, but Alex described it as insane. He showed her his bottle of psychiatric medication, again beaming with pride.

He explained this certificate gave him ADA protection, making it much more difficult for him to be fired.

A few months later, Jessica and Alex were working on a large project valued at over a million dollars. They had been negotiating for months, and the day came when the vendor was to arrive and the deal would be signed.

Jessica got a call from Alex that morning, "I need you to sign the contract."

"Excuse me?" Jessica was incredulous, thinking he was joking. He never allowed anyone to sign anything.

"I'm out today, finish the negotiations and sign the deal."

"Sure, boss," Jessica replied. She had learned a long time ago never to argue with the man.

Jessica arrived at the office an hour later and went out to the patio. Two large men, huge wrestler types, muscle-bound people wearing bullet-proof vests and carrying guns on their hips were standing, looking around alertly at everything and everyone.

What the hell? Jessica thought. She went back inside, making no sudden moves, grabbed one of her co-workers, and peeked out at the scene. Yep, there were two heavily armed men standing there.

As it turned out, Alex was going to be fired that day. Somehow he figured it out and called in sick. The guards were brought in as a precaution because he might be unstable.

This was the most extreme case of workplace instability I've ever encountered, but Alex represented a type of manager that exists in many organizations: the psychologically unstable boss whose mental health issues create chaos and fear for everyone around them.

Working for someone with untreated mental illness is extraordinarily difficult. You never know which version of your boss you're going to encounter on any given day. The person who gives you a huge raise in the morning might be screaming at you about a minor issue that afternoon.

Alex's behavior showed several warning signs of serious mental instability. His mood swings were extreme, swinging from grandiose generosity to angry micromanagement within hours. He was paranoid, isolating his department and controlling all communication to prevent his team from talking to anyone without his presence. His approval and denial of routine requests was completely unpredictable. He shared personal medical information inappropriately. And he used his psychiatric diagnosis not as motivation to seek treatment, but as a shield against accountability.

The most disturbing aspect was how Alex weaponized his mental illness. Rather than seeking treatment and managing his condition professionally, he used his psychiatric diagnosis as protection from accountability. He essentially told his employees that he was legally insane and there was nothing they could do about it.

This created an impossible working environment. How do you have a rational conversation with someone who proudly claims to be irrational? How do you reason with a boss who uses his mental illness as an excuse for erratic and damaging behavior?

The isolation he imposed on his department was particularly harmful. By preventing his team from communicating with other departments without his presence, he created an information silo that made collaboration nearly impossible. This wasn't protective management; it was controlling behavior that damaged the department's effectiveness and his employees' professional relationships.

The armed security guards were the final confirmation that the organization recognized Alex as a genuine threat. When your company feels the need to bring in armed protection because they're afraid of how a manager might react to being fired, you know the situation has moved far beyond normal workplace dysfunction.


If you find yourself working for someone who shows signs of serious psychological instability, prioritize your safety above all else. Document concerning behavior, don't try to manage their condition, and have an exit strategy ready. No job is worth risking your physical or mental wellbeing.


Jessica's experience shows how dangerous it can be when organizations fail to address mentally unstable managers. The company apparently knew Alex was problematic (hence the armed security), but they allowed the situation to continue until it required termination with security guards present.

This failure put all of Alex's employees at risk and created a toxic work environment that probably lasted months longer than necessary. The damage to department morale, productivity, and employee wellbeing was enormous and could have been avoided with earlier intervention.

Mental illness is a serious medical condition that deserves compassion and appropriate treatment. However, that doesn't mean employees should have to endure abuse, chaos, and potentially dangerous situations because their boss refuses to manage their condition professionally.

There's a difference between accommodating someone's mental health needs and allowing untreated psychological problems to terrorize an entire department. Alex crossed that line long before the company finally acted.

Working for a psychologically unstable boss is not a normal part of corporate life that you have to endure. If you find yourself in this situation, prioritize your safety and wellbeing over loyalty to your job or your boss.

No paycheck is worth working in fear or dealing with the chaos that comes from serious untreated mental illness in a position of authority. Find a safer environment where you can do your work without wondering whether your boss might snap at any moment.

The fact that a company needs armed security to fire someone should tell you everything you need to know about whether that person should have been managing people in the first place.

# Chapter 9: The Boss Is Hostile



Have you ever found yourself in a hostile work situation without understanding what was happening? Since Damien took pride in being competent, productive, and a good communicator, he had very few negative experiences with any boss. Sure, like everyone, he received the occasional correction or pointed discussion, but those were few and far between.

"What the hell is wrong with you?" Damien's new boss, who had only been on the job for a month, screamed at the top of his voice. Damien's subordinates looked over to see what was happening and wisely decided they needed to be somewhere else.

"Excuse me?" Damien said, keeping his temper under firm control. He'd been briefed by his peers about the new boss's tendency to fly off the handle and had already experienced his short fuse several times.

"You sent me an email," he snarled, "asking me for someone's name."

"And?" Damien said, still trying to figure out what was going on.

"Never do that again," the boss replied, loud enough for everyone to hear. "Do you understand me? You work for me, not the other way around. You do things for me. Got it?"

"Boss," Damien said, still not having a clue what was going on. He kept his voice completely even, emotions firmly under control. "Can we go into a conference room and discuss this? It's not appropriate for you to be screaming at me in the middle of the office."

He nodded, and the two of them proceeded to the nearby conference room. For the next sixty minutes, this man chewed Damien up one side and down the other, loud enough for everyone in the entire office to hear him.

This was the third time Damien had been chewed out by the new boss in less than a week. Damien felt his health suffering. He couldn't focus, and the feeling of being "caved-in" was profound.

Damien learned a lot from that episode in his life. He realized that no job, no matter the circumstances, was worth tolerating being abused.

An unpleasant workplace environment will result in a miserable life. After all, the job is usually vital to one's standard of living, survival, and feelings of self-worth.

So what do you do when the boss is actively hostile towards you, and it doesn't fall under protected categories like racial or sexual harassment?


What options are available for situations of verbal abuse?


When dealing with a hostile boss, stay calm and try to understand what's driving their behavior. If the situation can't be improved through direct communication, consider requesting a transfer or plan your exit. Your mental health is more important than any job.

In all cases of hostility from someone higher on the organizational chart, the subordinate is at a disadvantage. The hostile manager is abusing their power by creating a workplace that is unpleasant and unhealthy.

You should either fix the situation or leave. Maintaining employment in a hostile environment will make you sick, cause mental anguish, and negatively affect your whole life.

I've worked for several hostile bosses throughout my career, and the pattern is always the same. They create an atmosphere of fear and anxiety that poisons the entire workplace. People walk on eggshells, afraid to make any mistake that might trigger another explosion. Productivity suffers because everyone is more focused on avoiding confrontation than on doing good work.

The worst part about hostile bosses is the unpredictability. You never know what will set them off. Damien's boss exploded because he received an email asking for someone's name. That's not just unreasonable; it's completely irrational. How are you supposed to do your job if you can't ask basic questions without triggering a screaming fit?

Hostile bosses often use intimidation as a management tool. They believe that if they keep people scared, they'll work harder and make fewer mistakes. The opposite is true. Fear makes people less creative, less willing to take initiative, and more likely to make errors because they're operating in constant stress.

The public nature of Damien's humiliation was particularly damaging. When a boss screams at you in front of your colleagues and subordinates, it doesn't just hurt you. It undermines your authority and credibility with everyone who witnesses it. Your team sees you being treated like a child, and it becomes much harder to lead them effectively.

Some hostile bosses are equal opportunity abusers who treat everyone badly. Others seem to single out particular people for special treatment. Either way, the result is a toxic work environment where good people leave and those who stay become either beaten down or equally hostile themselves.

The physical and mental health effects of working for a hostile boss are real and serious. The constant stress can cause headaches, insomnia, digestive problems, and a weakened immune system. The psychological impact includes anxiety, depression, and a loss of confidence that can persist long after you leave that job.

Damien's realization that no job is worth being abused was exactly right. Your mental and physical health are more important than any paycheck. Your self-respect is more valuable than job security. Working for someone who screams at you and treats you with contempt will damage you in ways that go far beyond your professional life.

Hostile bosses often target people when they're most vulnerable. They wait until you're dependent on the job, maybe because of family obligations or financial pressures, and then ramp up the abuse because they know you can't easily leave.

This is why having an emergency fund and keeping your resume updated are so important. When you have options, you have power. When you're trapped in a job because you can't afford to leave, you become a victim.

Some people try to manage hostile bosses by figuring out their triggers and avoiding them. This is a mistake. You shouldn't have to become a student of someone else's psychological problems just to do your job. Trying to manage your manager's anger issues will consume enormous amounts of your time and energy while never actually solving the problem.

The best response to a hostile boss is what Damien eventually did: recognize that the situation is unacceptable and take steps to leave.

If you find yourself working for a hostile boss, start planning your exit immediately. Update your resume, activate your professional network, and begin looking for opportunities elsewhere. Don't wait for the situation to improve or hope that the boss will change. Hostile behavior is usually a character trait, not a temporary mood.

Document the hostile incidents in case you need evidence for unemployment claims or legal action, but don't count on HR or upper management to solve the problem. In most organizations, a boss has to do something really egregious before they face consequences for creating a hostile work environment.

No one should have to endure workplace hostility. When a manager uses anger and intimidation as management tools, they've revealed their incompetence. Find someone who leads through competence, not fear.

Hostile managers often follow predictable patterns. They typically target one person at a time, rotating their focus to keep everyone off balance. They escalate conflicts during stressful periods when they can blame their behavior on external pressures. They're often worse in private settings where there are no witnesses to their abuse.

I've noticed that hostile bosses frequently have enablers — colleagues or superiors who make excuses for their behavior. "That's just how he is," or "She's under a lot of pressure lately," or "He gets results, even if his methods are rough." These enablers allow the hostile behavior to continue by normalizing abuse and shifting blame to the victims.

The most dangerous aspect of working for a hostile boss is how it changes your own behavior. You start anticipating their moods, adjusting your communication style to avoid triggering outbursts, and walking on eggshells constantly. This hypervigilance is exhausting and can persist long after you leave that environment. Recovery involves relearning how to operate in normal, professional relationships where disagreement doesn't lead to verbal assault.

# Chapter 10: The Boss Is Sexually Harassing



The project was behind schedule, and Todd wanted to get it done so he could have the weekend free without worrying about it. He was at his desk working, even though it was 9 pm. He was alone in the building, busily typing away, solving some obscure coding issue.

Todd almost jumped out of his skin when he heard a loud banging behind him. He turned, his heart pumping and hands shaking, and saw Debra, the VP of HR, standing in the doorway. She had dropped her briefcase and bent over to pick it up.

She was not exactly dressed for the office. Todd guessed she had just come from a party. He said hello and turned back to work on his program. He wanted to get it done, and since it was getting late, Todd wasn't sure how much longer his brain was going to function.

A few minutes later, Todd felt hands on his shoulders and startled badly. Todd was your typical geeky programmer, and his focus was completely on his work. He had forgotten entirely that she was there.

Debra was massaging his shoulders.

"What are you doing?" Todd asked, turning to face her.

"You are way too tense," she said.

"Um," Todd replied, "Please stop. I'm trying to concentrate."

Todd turned back to his computer and started to type. She tapped him on the shoulder.

"I can help with that tension," she said.

"Debra," Todd said carefully, "you're married, and you are a Vice President. This isn't right."

"Screw that," she said.

"No," Todd replied, turning back to her. "Let's not go there."

"You're serious," she said. "I'm offering this," she indicated her body, "and you are turning me down?"

"Yes, I am," Todd said.

"Well," she said, "you could at least be polite about it."

Todd turned back, "You know, this is very ironic. Just a few weeks ago you gave a speech to the staff on sexual harassment. Please explain to me how this is different."

She looked at Todd, said, "Idiot," turned and left.

Todd expected to be fired. She was two levels above him on the organizational chart, and her husband was the CEO of the company. However, he never heard another word, although she tended to avoid him after that. Todd was just glad he didn't need human resources very often.

I witnessed another situation involving a different kind of sexual predator. Dwayne had a new boss named Sam. He was a nice enough guy, and reasonably competent. Dwayne liked working for him, for the most part, although something didn't seem quite right. It wasn't like there was anything wrong, it was more like Dwayne was missing something that everybody else knew.

"How are you today?" Sam asked one day while Dwayne was working.

"Very well, thanks," Dwayne replied. "The project is on-time, and that makes me happy."

"Well, good," he replied. "Hey, I wanted to ask you if you would like to get some lunch and have a drink with me?"

It wasn't unusual for him to invite members of his team to lunch, but there was something about his tone of voice...

"Um," Dwayne replied, "No, but thanks. I've got plans."

"You sure?" he asked. "We'll have fun."

Dwayne looked at his face, and then it hit him. He suddenly realized what he had missed and what everyone else in the office knew.

"Oh, well," Dwayne replied. He had no idea how to handle this. "Um, no."

"Why not?" he asked.

Dwayne sighed, "Sam, I like women."

He looked at Dwayne, "I know, but I thought you might..."

"No," Dwayne said, "and even if I didn't like women, you are my boss, and that's unacceptable."

After that day, it seemed Dwayne's reviews became more critical, he got chewed out more often, and he was assigned to the worst jobs.

These two stories show different aspects of workplace sexual harassment. In the first case, Debra used her position of power to make unwanted sexual advances on a subordinate who was alone and vulnerable. In the second case, Sam created a hostile work environment when his advances were rejected.

What both situations have in common is the abuse of power. Sexual harassment in the workplace is rarely about attraction or romance. It's about power and control. Predators target people who are in vulnerable positions, either because they're alone (like Todd) or because they depend on the harasser for their livelihood (like Dwayne).

Todd's situation was particularly egregious because Debra was the VP of Human Resources, the very person who was supposed to protect employees from this kind of behavior. Her hypocrisy was stunning. She had recently given a presentation on sexual harassment, then turned around and engaged in exactly the behavior she had warned others about.

The irony wasn't lost on Todd when he pointed out this contradiction. Her response, calling him an "idiot" for rejecting her advances, revealed her true character. She wasn't interested in his consent or comfort. She was used to getting what she wanted through her position of power.

Dwayne's situation shows how sexual harassment can escalate into workplace retaliation. When Sam's advances were rejected, he didn't accept the "no" gracefully. Instead, he punished Dwayne through negative performance reviews, increased criticism, and assignment to undesirable projects. This is a classic pattern of harassment followed by retaliation.

Both men handled their situations well, given the circumstances. Todd was direct in his rejection and pointed out the inappropriateness of the behavior. Dwayne was clear about his lack of interest and explicitly stated that the power dynamic made any relationship unacceptable.

However, both situations show how difficult it can be for victims of workplace sexual harassment to get justice. Todd expected to be fired because his harasser was married to the CEO. Dwayne experienced ongoing retaliation that probably affected his career advancement and job satisfaction.

Sexual harassment in the workplace takes many forms. It can be overt sexual advances like Debra's inappropriate touching and propositions. It can be persistent requests for dates despite clear rejections. It can involve sexual comments, jokes, or discussions that create an uncomfortable work environment. It can include the display of sexually explicit materials or images.

If you experience sexual harassment: clearly reject unwanted advances, document everything, report it immediately, and remember that harassment is never the victim's fault. The key is creating a paper trail and getting the behavior on record as soon as possible.

Seek support. Talk to trusted friends, family members, or a counselor about what you're experiencing. Consider contacting organizations that specialize in helping harassment victims.

Know your legal rights. Sexual harassment is illegal under federal law and the laws of most states. You may have grounds for a lawsuit, especially if the company fails to address the problem. (Consult with an employment attorney for advice specific to your situation, as harassment laws can be complex.)

If your company won't act, you can file complaints with the Equal Employment Opportunity Commission or your state's civil rights agency.

The most important thing to remember is that you have the right to work in an environment free from sexual harassment. No job is worth tolerating sexual abuse, and you shouldn't have to endure inappropriate behavior just to keep your paycheck.

Sexual harassment can have lasting effects on victims, including anxiety, depression, loss of confidence, and physical health problems. The workplace stress can affect your entire life, damaging relationships with family and friends.

Many companies fail to take sexual harassment seriously, especially when the harasser is in a position of power. HR departments may be more concerned with protecting the company from lawsuits than protecting employees from predators.

This is why external reporting and legal action are sometimes necessary. Companies that won't police themselves need external pressure to change their behavior.

Todd and Dwayne were fortunate that their harassment didn't escalate to physical assault or more severe retaliation. Not all victims are so lucky. Sexual harassment can escalate quickly, especially when the harasser feels emboldened by their position or by the victim's apparent vulnerability.

If you witness sexual harassment happening to a colleague, don't stay silent. Report what you've seen and offer to serve as a witness if the victim decides to file a complaint. Bystander intervention can be crucial in stopping harassment and supporting victims.

Sexual harassment is a serious problem that destroys careers, damages mental health, and creates toxic work environments. It's not harmless flirtation or compliments. It's an abuse of power that has no place in any workplace.

Every employee deserves to be treated with respect and dignity, regardless of their gender, sexual orientation, or position in the company hierarchy. When that basic standard isn't met, it's everyone's responsibility to speak up and take action.

# Chapter 11: The HR Reality Check



After thirty-three years in corporate America, I can say with complete confidence that Human Resources is not your friend. This isn't cynicism or bitterness talking. It's the hard truth learned from watching HR departments consistently protect bad managers while throwing good employees under the bus.

If you're reading this book because you're dealing with a toxic boss and thinking HR will save you, let me disabuse you of that notion right now. HR exists to protect the company from lawsuits, not to protect you from bad management.

I learned this lesson early in my career when I witnessed a situation that opened my eyes to how HR really operates.

Sarah was a solid performer who had been with the company for five years. Her new boss, Mike, took an immediate dislike to her for reasons that were never clear. Maybe she reminded him of someone he didn't like. Maybe he felt threatened by her knowledge of systems he didn't understand. Maybe he just needed a scapegoat for his own incompetence.

Whatever the reason, Mike began a campaign to make Sarah's life miserable. He excluded her from important meetings, then criticized her for not knowing what was discussed. He assigned her impossible deadlines, then wrote her up for missing them. He nitpicked her work to a degree that bordered on harassment.

Sarah documented everything. She kept copies of unreasonable emails, recorded instances of being excluded from meetings, and saved examples of the impossible tasks she was assigned. After three months of this treatment, she finally went to HR.

"I need to file a complaint about my supervisor," Sarah told the HR director.

"What seems to be the problem?" the HR director asked, her tone immediately defensive.

Sarah laid out the pattern of harassment, showing her documentation and explaining how her boss was creating a hostile work environment.

"Well," the HR director said after reviewing the materials, "it sounds like Mike is just trying to bring you up to his standards. Maybe you should focus on improving your performance rather than complaining about your supervisor."

Sarah was stunned. She had clear documentation of unreasonable treatment, but HR was dismissing her concerns and suggesting the problem was her performance.

"But look at these deadlines," Sarah said, pointing to an email where Mike had demanded a month-long project be completed in three days. "This isn't reasonable."

"Mike knows the business needs," the HR director replied. "If he says three days is enough time, then you need to find a way to make it work."

The meeting ended with HR telling Sarah they would "look into it" but making it clear they considered her concerns unfounded.

Two weeks later, Sarah was called into another HR meeting. This time, Mike was there too.

"Sarah," the HR director said, "Mike has brought some concerns to our attention about your attitude and performance. We're going to put you on a performance improvement plan."

Sarah looked at the papers they slid across the table. The PIP outlined vague performance issues and gave her thirty days to improve or face termination. Every complaint she had documented about Mike's unreasonable treatment was now being used as evidence of her failure to meet expectations.

"This is retaliation," Sarah said. "I filed a complaint two weeks ago, and now suddenly I'm on a performance improvement plan?"

"Your complaint was investigated," the HR director replied smoothly. "We found no evidence of inappropriate conduct. This PIP is based on legitimate performance concerns that Mike has documented over the past several months."

Sarah realized what had happened. The moment she filed her complaint, HR had gone to Mike and essentially told him to build a case against her. Instead of investigating her concerns about harassment, they had helped her harasser create documentation to fire her.

She was terminated thirty days later for "failure to meet performance expectations."

This is how HR really works. They don't investigate complaints to determine if managers are behaving badly. They investigate complaints to determine if those complaints pose a legal risk to the company. If they decide the complaint is unlikely to result in a successful lawsuit, they often work with the complained-about manager to eliminate the complainer.

I've seen this pattern repeated dozens of times throughout my career. An employee files a harassment complaint. HR conducts a perfunctory "investigation" that consists mainly of asking the accused manager for their side of the story. The manager denies everything and provides alternative explanations for their behavior. HR concludes there's insufficient evidence of wrongdoing. The complaining employee suddenly finds themselves under increased scrutiny, with their performance questioned and their future at the company in jeopardy.

The message is clear: don't complain, or you'll be the one who gets punished.

HR departments like to present themselves as neutral arbiters who are there to help resolve workplace conflicts. This is fiction. HR works for management, not for employees. Their job is to minimize the company's legal and financial exposure, even if that means sacrificing good employees to protect bad managers.

Why does this happen? The reasons stack up. Bad managers are often higher on the organizational chart than the employees who complain about them, so HR is more likely to side with whoever has more power and influence. Firing a manager creates far more disruption than firing an individual contributor — replacing one employee is simply easier than dealing with the fallout of removing a leader. Admitting that harassment occurred also opens the company to legal liability, since acknowledging wrongdoing is essentially admitting fault.

Beyond that, many HR professionals genuinely lack the stomach to confront powerful managers; they chose their careers to avoid conflict, not wade into it. And finally, HR performance metrics are typically based on keeping complaint numbers low and avoiding legal settlements. An HR director who makes problems disappear — even by eliminating the complainers — looks good on paper.

This doesn't mean you should never go to HR. Sometimes you have no choice, especially if you're dealing with clearly illegal behavior like sexual harassment or racial discrimination. But you should go in with realistic expectations and a clear understanding of whose interests HR is really protecting.

If you do decide to involve HR, go in prepared. Document everything obsessively before and after any HR conversations, and assume HR will share whatever you tell them with the person you're complaining about. Focus your complaint on behavior that's clearly illegal or violates specific company policies — vague complaints about "poor management" or "unfair treatment" are easy to dismiss. Follow up every conversation with HR with a written email summary of what was discussed and what actions were promised.

Be prepared for retaliation. Filing a complaint often makes the immediate situation worse before it gets better. Have an exit strategy ready in case the process goes sideways. And know that sometimes going directly to the EEOC, your state's civil rights agency, or an employment lawyer is more effective than anything HR will do. Keep your expectations low — HR's job is to protect the company, not to fix bad managers or make you happy.

The most important thing to understand is that HR is not a neutral party in workplace disputes. They are advocates for the company, and they will act in whatever way they believe best serves the company's interests. Sometimes that means protecting employees, but more often it means protecting managers and minimizing potential legal exposure.

Sarah's story isn't unusual. It's the norm. Good employees who complain about bad managers often find themselves pushed out of their jobs while the bad managers continue their destructive behavior with impunity.

This is why building your own exit strategy is so much more important than hoping HR will solve your problems. Update your resume, build your professional network, save money for a potential job transition, and be prepared to leave if necessary.

Don't waste months or years trying to work within a broken system. If you're dealing with a toxic manager and HR won't help (and they probably won't), start planning your escape. Life is too short to spend it hoping that people whose job is to protect the company will somehow decide to protect you instead.

The system is not designed to help good employees deal with bad managers. The sooner you accept this reality, the sooner you can take control of your own career and find a better place to work.

# Chapter 12: Documentation, Your Only Real Protection

---

*"In God we trust. All others must bring data." — W. Edwards Deming*

---

After dealing with toxic bosses for over three decades, I've learned one fundamental truth: your memory means nothing, your word means nothing, and witness testimony means nothing. The only thing that matters in workplace disputes is what you can prove with documentation.

I learned this lesson the hard way when I tried to challenge a manager's behavior without proper evidence to back up my claims.

My boss, Frank, had a pattern of making promises in verbal conversations and then denying he'd ever made them. He would agree to budget increases in meetings, then claim he never approved the spending. He would promise promotions and raises to team members, then act surprised when they brought up his commitments.

The breaking point came when Frank promised our entire team bonuses for completing a critical project ahead of schedule and under budget. We busted our asses for three months, working nights and weekends to meet his aggressive timeline. When we delivered the project two weeks early and 15% under budget, we were proud of what we'd accomplished.

"Great work, everyone," Frank announced at our team meeting. "I'll make sure those bonuses we discussed are in your next paychecks."

Two weeks later, no bonuses appeared. When I approached Frank about it, he looked at me like I was crazy.

"Bonuses? I never promised any bonuses. You must have misunderstood."

"Frank, you specifically told us there would be bonuses for early completion."

"I think you're confused," he replied. "We discussed possible future bonuses if the company performs well this year, but I never made any specific commitments."

I was furious but powerless. It was my word against his, and he was two levels above me in the organization. When I brought it up with other team members, they all remembered the promise but were afraid to speak up against a manager who controlled their careers.

That's when I realized that verbal agreements and promises are worthless when dealing with dishonest managers. From that day forward, I documented everything.

Every important conversation gets followed up with an email. After every meeting or phone call where decisions are made or commitments given, I send a summary email. "Hi Frank, just wanted to confirm what we discussed in today's meeting. You agreed to approve the $50,000 equipment purchase and said the bonuses for early project completion would be processed by month-end. Please let me know if I misunderstood anything."

Most of the time, managers don't respond to these emails, which creates a paper trail showing they didn't dispute your version of events. Occasionally, they'll correct something in writing, which is even better because now you have their actual position documented.

Save everything. Every email, every text message, every written instruction or policy document. Create folders on your personal email account (not your work email) and forward important communications to yourself. Take photos of handwritten notes or documents with your phone.

I keep a work journal where I record significant events, conversations, and decisions. I write entries the same day things happen, while the details are fresh in my memory. The journal includes dates, times, locations, and names of witnesses when possible.

When documenting problematic behavior, I focus on specific, observable actions rather than interpretations or feelings. Instead of writing "Frank was being unreasonable," I write "Frank rejected the budget proposal and said the $10,000 expense was 'ridiculous' despite the fact that similar expenses had been approved three times in the past six months."

I learned to be particularly careful about documenting promises and commitments. When a manager makes a verbal promise, I follow up immediately with an email confirmation. This forces them to either confirm the promise in writing or clarify what they actually meant.

The key is creating contemporaneous records. Documentation created weeks or months after events looks suspicious and carries less weight than records made at the time things happened. Courts and employment agencies give much more credibility to evidence that was created as events unfolded.

I also learned to document patterns, not just individual incidents. One unreasonable request might be dismissed as poor judgment. Five unreasonable requests in two weeks establishes a pattern of harassment or incompetence.

When dealing with hostile or abusive behavior, I document the impact on my work and health. "After today's meeting where Frank yelled at me for 20 minutes about the client presentation, I had difficulty concentrating for the rest of the day and was unable to complete the quarterly report as scheduled."

Screenshots are invaluable. Email headers show when messages were sent and received. Screenshots of text messages capture the full conversation thread. Photos of whiteboards or documents preserve information that might disappear.

I keep backup copies of everything in multiple locations. Important documents are stored on my personal computer, backed up to cloud storage, and sometimes printed and kept in a secure location at home. You never know when you might lose access to your work computer or email.

The most important lesson I learned is that documentation must be started immediately, not after problems escalate. By the time you realize you need evidence, it's often too late to build a comprehensive case. The best documentation is created as part of your regular work routine, not as a reaction to specific problems.

This approach saved me twice when managers tried to rewrite history or blame me for their failures. In one case, a boss tried to claim I had never completed a project he'd cancelled midway through. My email trail showed his original approval, my progress updates, and his cancellation order. Without that documentation, it would have been my word against his.

In another situation, a manager tried to give me a negative performance review based on missed deadlines that were actually caused by his constantly changing priorities. My documentation showed the timeline of his changing instructions and how each change affected project schedules. The review was withdrawn.

Documentation also protects you during layoffs and restructuring. I've seen good employees fired because managers claimed their work was unsatisfactory, when the real reason was politics or budget cuts. Detailed records of your accomplishments, positive feedback, and successful project completions make it much harder for dishonest managers to manufacture performance problems.

The psychological benefit of good documentation is almost as important as the legal protection. When you know you have detailed records of everything that happens, you feel more confident in challenging inappropriate behavior. You're less likely to second-guess yourself when a manager tries to gaslight you about past events.

However, be smart about how you document things. Don't create records on company systems that your employer can delete or modify. Don't be obvious about documenting everything, as some managers will see this as a threat. And never fabricate or exaggerate events to make your case stronger. Good documentation is truthful, specific, and complete.

Some managers actually appreciate employees who document well because it helps them keep track of decisions and commitments. The only managers who object to documentation are those who plan to lie about what happened later.

Good documentation habits take time and effort, but they're the best investment you can make in your professional protection. In a world where your word means nothing and memories are unreliable, paper trails and digital records are your only defense against dishonest managers and dysfunctional organizations.

Start documenting today. You'll be glad you did when you need to prove what really happened.

# Chapter 13: Managing Up When Your Boss is Broken



Sometimes you find yourself in a situation where you can't immediately leave a toxic boss, but you still need to get your work done and protect your team. This requires a delicate balance: managing up to a dysfunctional manager without enabling their bad behavior or compromising your own integrity.

I learned this skill out of necessity when I worked for a boss named Marcus who was fundamentally incompetent but politically untouchable. He had been hired by the CEO and was widely known to be someone's nephew or college buddy. Despite his obvious shortcomings, he wasn't going anywhere, and neither was I for at least another eighteen months.

Marcus had several problems that made him nearly impossible to work for. He couldn't make decisions, constantly changed his mind about priorities, and had no understanding of the technical work our team was doing. He would commit us to impossible deadlines without consulting anyone, then disappear when it came time to explain why we couldn't meet them.

The breaking point came when Marcus promised a client we would deliver a complex software integration in three weeks. The project normally would have taken three months, and that was with everything going perfectly. When I tried to explain this to him, he just said, "Figure it out. That's what I'm paying you for."

I realized I had two obvious choices: let the project fail spectacularly and watch my team take the blame, or work eighty-hour weeks trying to deliver the impossible. I rejected both.

Instead, I managed up strategically while protecting my team from his dysfunction.

Give them what they need to look good, but on your terms. Marcus needed to tell the client that progress was being made, so I started sending him weekly status reports that he could forward up the chain. The reports were written in language that sounded impressive but didn't commit us to anything impossible. Instead of saying "the project will be completed on schedule," I wrote "significant progress has been made on core functionality with iterative improvements being implemented according to agile methodology."

Control the flow of information. Marcus had a tendency to panic and make rash decisions when he got incomplete information. So I made sure he only received carefully prepared updates that wouldn't send him into crisis mode. I would anticipate his questions and concerns and address them proactively in my communications.

Build relationships above and around him. I started having informal conversations with Marcus's peers and his boss about technical challenges and resource needs. I never complained about Marcus directly, but I made sure other leaders understood the constraints we were working under. When decisions needed to be made that Marcus couldn't or wouldn't make, I had alternative paths to get approvals.

Protect my team from his chaos. When Marcus would burst into our area with some new emergency or completely changed priorities, I became a buffer. I would listen to his latest crisis, tell him we'd address it immediately, and then translate his panic into reasonable work assignments for my team. My people learned that Marcus's emergencies weren't necessarily real emergencies, and they could focus on the actual work that needed to be done.

Document everything carefully. With a boss who constantly changed his mind and forgot what he'd said, documentation was crucial. But I had to be strategic about it. Instead of sending confrontational emails like "you said X but now you're saying Y," I would send helpful summary emails: "Based on our discussion, I understand the new priority is A instead of B. I'll redirect the team accordingly and update the timeline."

Make him think solutions were his idea. Marcus had a fragile ego and would reject good ideas if he thought they made him look bad. So I learned to present options in a way that let him take credit for the smart choice. Instead of saying "we should do X because Y," I would say "I've been thinking about what you said yesterday about Z, and I wonder if we might consider X as a way to achieve that."

The three-week software integration project is a perfect example of how this approach worked. I knew we couldn't deliver the full system, but I also knew the client really just needed core functionality to get started. I broke the project down into phases and identified what we could actually deliver in three weeks.

Then I went to Marcus and said, "I've been thinking about your strategy of impressing the client with quick results. What if we delivered Phase One ahead of schedule and positioned it as exceeding expectations by delivering early rather than trying to cram everything into the original timeline?"

Marcus loved this approach because it let him take credit for strategic thinking. The client was happy because they got something useful ahead of when they expected it. My team didn't have to work impossible hours on an impossible deadline. And I had managed to turn Marcus's incompetent promise into a reasonable project plan.

This approach isn't about enabling bad managers or making their dysfunction your problem to solve. It's about creating space for good work to happen despite their limitations. The key is maintaining your own standards and protecting your team while giving the broken boss what they need to stay out of your way.

There are some important boundaries to maintain when managing up to a dysfunctional boss. Don't lie for them or help them deceive others about problems. Don't take on responsibilities that are rightfully theirs, especially if it means working unreasonable hours to compensate for their failures. Don't let them abuse you or your team just because you're trying to make the situation workable.

The goal is to create stability and predictability in an unstable situation, not to become an enabler of bad management. Sometimes this means letting them fail at things that aren't your responsibility while protecting the work that is important to you and your team.

Managing up also means knowing when to escalate issues that the broken boss can't or won't handle. If there are safety concerns, legal issues, or problems that could seriously damage the company, you have an obligation to bring them to someone who can actually address them. Don't let loyalty to your team or desire to avoid confrontation prevent you from raising serious issues.

The most important thing to remember is that this is a temporary strategy, not a permanent solution. Managing up to a broken boss is exhausting and ultimately unsustainable. It requires you to do your job and part of theirs, which isn't fair and won't advance your career in the long run.

While you're managing up, you should also be planning your exit. Update your resume, build relationships with other leaders in the organization, and look for opportunities to transfer to a different department or find a new job entirely. Use the time you buy yourself through effective managing up to create better long-term options.

Marcus eventually was moved to a different role where he could do less damage, but not before I had found a better position elsewhere. The skills I learned in managing up to him served me well throughout my career, both in dealing with other difficult bosses and in understanding what not to do when I became a manager myself.

Managing up when your boss is broken isn't about fixing them or enabling their dysfunction. It's about creating enough stability and sanity to do good work while you figure out your next move. It's a survival skill, not a career strategy, and it should be used accordingly.

# Chapter 14: Exit Strategy Planning

*"It is not the man who has too little, but the man who craves more, who is poor." — Seneca*

The most important career advice I can give you is this: always be prepared to leave. Not because you're planning to quit tomorrow, but because having options gives you power. When you can afford to walk away from a toxic boss or dysfunctional company, you're no longer trapped by your circumstances.

I learned this lesson during one of the most stressful periods of my career, when I was working for a company that was slowly circling the drain. The management was incompetent, the finances were shaky, and morale was at rock bottom. Every day felt like a grind, but like many of my colleagues, I stayed because I needed the paycheck and didn't think I had anywhere else to go.

The wake-up call came during a particularly brutal week when my boss, Janet, decided to make me the scapegoat for a project that had failed due to her poor planning and impossible timeline. She called me into her office and spent forty-five minutes berating me for problems that were largely beyond my control.

"Your performance has been completely unacceptable," she said, waving a folder of documents. "I'm putting you on a performance improvement plan, and if I don't see immediate changes, you'll be looking for work elsewhere."

As I sat there being dressed down for failures that weren't mine, I realized something important: I was only tolerating this abuse because I felt like I had no choice. I had bills to pay, a mortgage, and barely enough savings to last a month without income. Janet knew this, and she was using my financial vulnerability to treat me like garbage.

That night, I went home and did something I should have done years earlier: I created a comprehensive exit strategy.

The foundation of any exit strategy is financial preparation. You need enough money saved to survive without income for at least six months, preferably longer. This isn't just about basic living expenses. You need to account for health insurance, continued mortgage or rent payments, and the costs associated with job searching.

I started by calculating my absolute minimum monthly expenses. Not what I was used to spending, but what I could survive on if necessary. I cut out all discretionary spending and started putting every extra dollar into a separate savings account I called my "escape fund."

Within eighteen months, I had saved enough money to last eight months without income. The psychological effect was immediate and profound. Knowing I could walk away from Janet's abuse changed everything about how I dealt with her. I stopped taking her criticism personally because I knew it wasn't really about my performance. I became calmer in our meetings because I wasn't desperate to keep her happy.

But financial preparation is only part of exit strategy planning. You also need to keep your professional options open and your skills current.

I updated my resume every six months, whether I was looking for a job or not. I kept track of my accomplishments, quantified my achievements, and made sure I could articulate the value I brought to any organization. I also started building relationships with recruiters in my field, not because I was actively looking, but because I wanted them to know who I was when the time came.

Networking became a regular part of my routine. I attended industry conferences, joined professional associations, and made an effort to stay in touch with former colleagues who had moved on to other companies. I learned that most good jobs are never advertised publicly. They're filled through networks and referrals, which means your next opportunity is likely to come from someone you know.

I also invested in keeping my skills current. Technology changes rapidly, and what was advanced five years ago might be obsolete today. I took online courses, earned certifications, and volunteered for projects that would expose me to new technologies and methodologies. The goal was to make sure I was always marketable, regardless of what happened with my current employer.

Professional reputation management became another priority. I started writing articles for industry publications, speaking at local meetups, and contributing to online forums where potential employers might see my expertise. I wanted to be known in my field, not just at my current company.

The exit strategy also included practical considerations that many people overlook. I made sure I had copies of all my important work product saved to personal storage. Not confidential company information, but examples of my work that I could use in portfolio presentations or to demonstrate my capabilities to potential employers.

I also started paying attention to my company's policies around non-compete agreements, confidentiality clauses, and stock options. I wanted to understand what restrictions might apply if I left and what benefits I might be forfeiting. This information would be crucial in negotiating any future departure.

Health insurance was another major consideration. I researched COBRA options and looked into individual health insurance plans so I would know what my options were if I needed to leave quickly. I also made sure I was up to date on all medical and dental checkups while I still had good insurance coverage.

The most important part of exit strategy planning is mental preparation. I started thinking of myself as an independent professional who happened to be working at this company, rather than as someone whose identity was tied to my current job. This shift in mindset was liberating.

I also began setting boundaries that I had been too scared to set before. When Janet would try to dump last-minute projects on me on Friday afternoons, I started pushing back. When she would make unreasonable demands, I would ask for clarification and confirmation in writing. I stopped working unpaid overtime to compensate for her poor planning.

The beautiful thing about having a solid exit strategy is that it often makes leaving unnecessary. Once I stopped acting desperate and started setting reasonable boundaries, Janet's behavior toward me improved significantly. She still wasn't a good manager, but she stopped using me as her personal stress relief target.

More importantly, other people in the organization started noticing my changed demeanor. I was more confident, more assertive, and more willing to speak up in meetings. Within a year, I was offered a promotion to a different department with a better manager and significantly better pay.

I didn't end up using my exit strategy to leave that company, but having it gave me the freedom to perform better and advocate for myself more effectively. The confidence that comes from knowing you have options is invaluable in any workplace situation.

However, there are times when you do need to execute your exit strategy quickly. I watched several colleagues get fired during layoffs who were completely unprepared. They had no savings, no current resumes, and no professional networks. They were forced to take the first job they could find, often at lower pay and worse conditions than what they had left.

If you're dealing with a toxic boss or dysfunctional organization, don't wait until the situation becomes unbearable to start planning your exit. Start building your escape fund today. Update your resume this week. Reach out to someone in your professional network this month.

The goal isn't to become a job hopper or to approach every workplace relationship with cynicism. The goal is to ensure that you're always working by choice, not by desperation. When you know you can leave, you're free to do your best work and stand up for yourself when necessary.

An exit strategy isn't just about leaving bad situations. It's about creating the freedom to pursue better opportunities when they arise. Some of the best career moves I've made happened because I was prepared to move quickly when the right opportunity presented itself.

Start planning your exit strategy today, even if you love your current job. You never know when circumstances might change, and by then it might be too late to prepare properly. The best time to build your escape fund is when you don't need it.

# Chapter 15: Building Boss-Proof Skills



The best defense against bad bosses is making yourself so valuable and marketable that you never have to depend on any single manager for your career success. When you have skills that are in demand and a reputation that precedes you, toxic bosses become temporary inconveniences rather than career-ending threats.

I learned this lesson after spending too many years feeling trapped by circumstances beyond my control. I was skilled at my specific job but had allowed my expertise to become narrow and company-specific. When layoffs came, I watched colleagues with broader skill sets land new positions quickly while I struggled to even get interviews.

The wake-up call came when I was passed over for a promotion that should have been mine. My boss, Eric, gave the job to his golf buddy despite the fact that I was clearly more qualified and had been doing half the work already. When I asked for feedback, Eric told me I was "too specialized" and needed to "broaden my horizons" if I wanted to advance.

That stung, but it was also the push I needed to take control of my professional development instead of waiting for my employer to invest in me.

I started by taking an honest inventory of my skills. What could I do that was valuable to other companies? What knowledge did I have that was transferable across industries? Where were the gaps in my expertise that made me vulnerable to economic shifts or organizational changes?

The analysis was sobering. Most of my knowledge was tied to proprietary systems and processes that were specific to my current employer. If I lost my job, I would be starting over in many ways. I had become what I now call "institutionally dependent," someone whose value was tied more to knowing how things worked at one particular company than to possessing broadly applicable skills.

I decided to change that systematically.

First, I started learning technologies and methodologies that were industry standards rather than company-specific solutions. Instead of becoming an expert in our internal database system, I learned SQL and database design principles that would apply anywhere. Instead of mastering our custom reporting tools, I learned Excel, PowerBI, and other widely-used business intelligence software.

The goal wasn't to abandon my current responsibilities but to ensure that everything I learned had applications beyond my current job. When Eric asked me to automate a manual process, I used it as an opportunity to learn Python scripting. When we needed to improve our project management, I got certified in Agile methodologies that were being used across the industry.

I also started paying attention to trends in my field and adjacent areas. What skills were becoming more important? What technologies were companies starting to adopt? What kinds of problems were businesses trying to solve? I read industry publications, followed thought leaders on social media, and attended webinars and conferences to stay current.

The key was being strategic about skill development. I didn't try to learn everything. Instead, I focused on building expertise in areas that were growing in demand and that complemented my existing strengths. I built deep expertise in one core area while developing working knowledge across several related ones.

Within two years, my LinkedIn profile was getting attention from recruiters on a regular basis. Not because I was actively job hunting, but because I had skills that were in demand and I had made those skills visible through my online presence.

This transformation had an immediate impact on my relationship with Eric. When you know that other companies want to hire you, it's much easier to stand up to unreasonable demands and push back against unfair treatment. I stopped working unpaid overtime to compensate for Eric's poor planning. I started saying no to projects that were outside my job description without corresponding increases in compensation.

Eric noticed the change in my attitude, and initially he didn't like it. But when he realized that I had become more valuable to the organization and that losing me would create real problems for him, his behavior toward me improved significantly. He started treating me more like a business partner and less like a subordinate he could take for granted.

The most important part of building boss-proof skills is developing what I call "portable expertise." These are capabilities that create value regardless of where you work or who you work for.

Problem-solving skills are universally valuable. Every organization has challenges that need solutions, and people who can analyze complex situations and develop effective approaches are always in demand. I practiced this by volunteering for cross-functional projects and taking on problems that other people avoided.

Communication skills are equally important. The ability to explain technical concepts to non-technical audiences, to write clearly and persuasively, and to support productive meetings is valuable in any organization. I improved these skills by writing internal documentation, presenting at team meetings, and eventually speaking at industry events.

Project management capabilities are essential in almost every role. Knowing how to plan work, manage resources, track progress, and deliver results on time and on budget is valuable regardless of your job title or industry. I got formal training in project management methodologies and applied them to everything I worked on.

Leadership skills matter even if you're not in a management position. The ability to influence others, build consensus, and drive initiatives forward makes you valuable to any organization. I developed these skills by taking on informal leadership roles in cross-departmental initiatives and professional associations.

I also focused on building what economists call "human capital," the combination of skills, experience, and relationships that makes you valuable in the job market. This meant not just learning new things but also documenting and communicating my accomplishments in ways that would be meaningful to potential employers.

I started keeping a detailed record of my achievements, quantifying the impact of my work whenever possible. Instead of just saying I "improved efficiency," I could say I "automated manual processes that saved 20 hours per week and reduced error rates by 35%." Instead of claiming I "enhanced customer satisfaction," I could demonstrate that my improvements "increased customer retention by 12% and reduced support tickets by 40%."

This documentation served two purposes. It made my annual performance reviews much easier because I had concrete examples of my contributions. More importantly, it gave me compelling stories to tell in job interviews and networking conversations.

Boss-proof skills also meant developing multiple revenue streams and professional relationships outside my current job. I started doing consulting work on weekends, not because I needed the money but because it exposed me to different industries and business models. This side work also served as a safety net and gave me additional credibility in my field.

I joined professional associations and started building relationships with people at other companies. These connections provided market intelligence about what skills were in demand, what companies were hiring, and what salary ranges were realistic for someone with my background.

The transformation wasn't immediate, but it was profound. Within three years, I had gone from feeling trapped by my circumstances to feeling confident about my professional options. When Eric eventually left the company and was replaced by someone even worse, I was able to transition to a better role at a different organization within six weeks.

The new position came with a 40% salary increase and significantly better working conditions. More importantly, I had learned that my career success didn't depend on the whims of any particular manager. I had skills that were valuable to multiple employers and relationships that could open doors when I needed them.

Boss-proof skills aren't about preparing to leave your current job. They're about ensuring that you're working by choice rather than by necessity. When you know you have options, you can focus on doing your best work instead of managing your manager's moods and political games.

Start building your boss-proof skills today. Identify the gaps in your expertise that make you vulnerable. Invest in learning technologies and methodologies that are industry standards. Build relationships outside your current organization. Document your achievements in ways that demonstrate measurable value.

The goal is to become the kind of professional that companies compete to hire rather than someone who competes desperately for jobs. When you reach that point, bad bosses become temporary inconveniences rather than career-defining threats.

# Chapter 16: Mental Health and Recovery

---

*"Your mental health is more important than your career, your bank account, and the opinions of others." — Mel Robbins*

---

Working for toxic bosses doesn't just damage your career. It damages you as a person. The constant stress, anxiety, and abuse take a real toll on your mental and physical health in ways that can persist long after you've escaped the situation. Understanding and addressing this damage is crucial for your long-term wellbeing.

I learned this lesson the hard way after working for a boss named Karen who turned what should have been an exciting new job into a psychological nightmare. Karen was a master manipulator who used fear, intimidation, and emotional abuse to control her staff. She would praise you one day and tear you down the next, keeping everyone off balance and desperate for her approval.

The job started well. Karen was charming during the interview process, speaking passionately about teamwork and professional development. She painted a picture of an environment where I could grow and make meaningful contributions to the organization. The reality was completely different.

Within my first month, I realized that Karen's management style was based on keeping people insecure and competing for her favor. She would give contradictory instructions to different team members, then act surprised when conflicts arose. She would promise opportunities and resources that never materialized, then blame others for "misunderstanding" what she had said.

The worst part was how she would single out people for public humiliation. During team meetings, she would spend twenty or thirty minutes dissecting someone's work, pointing out every minor flaw while the rest of us sat there grateful it wasn't our turn. These sessions weren't about improving performance. They were about demonstrating her power and keeping everyone afraid.

I tried to adapt by working harder and being more careful with my work. I double-checked everything, stayed late to ensure projects were perfect, and walked on eggshells around Karen to avoid triggering one of her outbursts. Nothing helped. No matter how much effort I put in, she would find something to criticize.

The stress started affecting me in ways I didn't initially recognize. I began having trouble sleeping, waking up at 3 AM thinking about work problems that probably weren't even real. I lost my appetite and dropped fifteen pounds without trying. I became irritable with my family and withdrew from friends because I was too exhausted to maintain social relationships.

Most troubling was how I started doubting myself. Karen was so skilled at manipulation that I began to wonder if maybe I really was incompetent. Maybe I wasn't cut out for this type of work. Maybe her criticism was justified and I was just too defensive to see it.

This self-doubt is one of the most insidious effects of psychological abuse in the workplace. When someone in authority constantly tells you that your work is inadequate, your judgment is poor, and your contributions are worthless, you start to believe it. Your confidence erodes until you question every decision you make.

After six months of this treatment, I was a wreck. I dreaded going to work each morning and would sit in my car in the parking lot for ten or fifteen minutes, trying to gather the courage to walk into the building. I started having what I now recognize as anxiety attacks, episodes where my heart would race and I would feel like I couldn't breathe.

The breaking point came during one of Karen's public humiliation sessions. She spent forty-five minutes picking apart a presentation I had given, questioning not just the content but my competence and professionalism. As she spoke, I felt something snap inside me. I realized that no job was worth this level of abuse.

I quit that day without having another position lined up. It was financially risky, but I knew I had to get away from Karen before she destroyed what was left of my confidence and self-respect.

The recovery process took much longer than I expected. Even after leaving that toxic environment, I continued to experience symptoms of what I now understand was workplace trauma. I would have nightmares about Karen calling me into her office. I would second-guess decisions that previously would have been routine for me. I would feel anxious in meetings with new managers, waiting for them to start attacking my work.

It took several months of therapy to understand what had happened to me. My therapist explained that prolonged exposure to psychological abuse in the workplace can create symptoms similar to post-traumatic stress disorder. The constant hypervigilance, the fear of making mistakes, the erosion of self-confidence are all normal responses to abnormal treatment.

The healing process involved several important steps. First, I had to accept that what I had experienced was abuse, not just "tough management" or "high standards." Karen's behavior was deliberately harmful and designed to maintain her power over others. Recognizing this helped me stop blaming myself for the problems in that workplace.

Second, I had to rebuild my confidence systematically. I started by taking on small freelance projects where I could demonstrate my competence to myself and receive positive feedback from clients. Each successful project helped counter the negative messages that Karen had drilled into my head.

Third, I had to relearn how to trust my own judgment. Working for Karen had trained me to constantly seek external validation and approval. I had to practice making decisions without immediately wondering if I was doing something wrong.

The physical symptoms took time to resolve as well. It took months before I could sleep through the night consistently. My appetite returned gradually as the constant stress decreased. The anxiety attacks became less frequent and eventually stopped altogether.

One of the most important things I learned is that seeking professional help is not a sign of weakness. Therapy gave me tools to process what had happened and strategies for preventing future toxic work situations from affecting me as severely. A good therapist can help you distinguish between reasonable workplace stress and psychological abuse.

I also learned to pay attention to early warning signs in future jobs. Managers who are overly critical during the interview process, who speak negatively about former employees, or who seem to thrive on conflict are red flags. Workplaces where people seem afraid to speak up or where there's high turnover in certain departments deserve scrutiny.

The recovery process also taught me the importance of maintaining perspective about work. Your job is important, but it's not your identity. A bad boss's opinion of you doesn't define your worth as a person or a professional. When work becomes the primary source of stress and unhappiness in your life, it's time to make changes.

I wish I could say that my experience with Karen was unique, but I've met many people with similar stories. Psychological abuse in the workplace is more common than most people realize, and its effects can be severe and long-lasting. The victims often blame themselves, which compounds the damage and makes recovery more difficult.

If you're currently dealing with a toxic boss, please understand that the stress you're feeling is real and valid. Don't minimize the impact that psychological abuse is having on your health and wellbeing. Don't tell yourself that you should be able to handle it better or that you're being too sensitive.

Take care of your physical and mental health. Get regular exercise, maintain social connections outside of work, and consider talking to a counselor or therapist about what you're experiencing. Don't let shame prevent you from seeking help. Professional support can make an enormous difference in how you cope with and recover from workplace trauma.

Most importantly, have an exit plan. As I learned from my experience with Karen, sometimes the only solution is to leave. No amount of money or career advancement is worth sacrificing your mental health. There are better jobs and better managers out there, but you won't find them if you're too damaged to recognize them or pursue them.

The workplace doesn't have to be a source of trauma and stress. You deserve to work in an environment where you're treated with respect and where your contributions are valued. Don't settle for less, and don't let toxic managers convince you that abuse is normal or that you deserve poor treatment.

Recovery from workplace trauma is possible, but it requires acknowledging what happened, seeking appropriate help, and making changes to prevent it from happening again. Your mental health is too important to sacrifice for any job or any boss.

# Chapter 17: Leading Differently



After thirty-three years of working for various disasters, I eventually became a manager myself. The question was whether I would repeat the patterns of dysfunction I had experienced or use those negative examples to build something better. I wish I could say I got it right immediately, but the truth is that learning to be a good leader after experiencing so much bad leadership was harder than I expected.

My first management role came when I was promoted to lead a team of six software developers. I was excited about the opportunity but nervous about the responsibility. I had clear ideas about what I didn't want to do based on all the toxic bosses I had endured, but figuring out what I should do instead was more challenging.

My biggest mistake in those early months was overcorrecting. I had worked for so many micromanagers that I swung too far in the opposite direction, giving my team almost no guidance or oversight. I thought I was being respectful of their autonomy, but what I was actually doing was abandoning my responsibilities as a leader.

The wake-up call came during a project review meeting with senior management. My team had been working for two months on what should have been a straightforward system upgrade, but they had gotten bogged down in technical debates and scope creep. When my boss asked for a status update, I realized I didn't really know where things stood because I had been so hands-off.

"We're making good progress," I said, hoping that was actually true. "The team is working through some technical challenges, but we should be on track for the original deadline."

After the meeting, I went back to my team to get a real status update. What I discovered was that they had spent weeks debating the best approach without making any actual decisions. They had built several prototypes but hadn't committed to any of them. They were confused about the requirements because I hadn't provided clear guidance about priorities and constraints.

The project was at least a month behind schedule, and nobody had told me because I had created an environment where they didn't think they needed to keep me informed.

That's when I realized that being a good manager isn't just about avoiding the mistakes of bad managers. You also have to actually manage, which means making decisions, providing direction, and maintaining accountability.

I called a team meeting and admitted my mistake. "I've been so focused on not micromanaging you that I haven't been managing at all," I told them. "That's not fair to you, and it's not good for the project. We need to change how we're working together."

I spent the next week having one-on-one conversations with each team member to understand their perspective on what wasn't working and what they needed from me as their manager. The feedback was illuminating and humbling.

They wanted clear priorities and decision-making authority when they disagreed about technical approaches. They wanted regular check-ins to discuss obstacles and get guidance, but not constant interference in their daily work. They wanted to know how their work fit into the bigger picture and why it mattered to the organization.

Most importantly, they wanted to feel like they had a manager who was engaged and supportive, not absent or indifferent.

Based on this feedback, I developed what became my management philosophy over the years. Set clear expectations and priorities, then give people the freedom to figure out how to meet them. Be available for guidance and support, but don't hover over people while they work. Make decisions promptly when your team needs direction, but let them make decisions within their areas of expertise.

I also learned the importance of regular communication. I instituted brief weekly one-on-ones with each team member, not to check up on their work but to understand what obstacles they were facing and how I could help remove them. These conversations became invaluable for catching problems early and maintaining strong working relationships.

One of the most important things I learned was how to give feedback effectively. I had experienced so many managers who either never provided feedback or delivered it in destructive ways. I realized that good feedback is specific, timely, and focused on helping people improve rather than making them feel bad about mistakes.

When someone on my team made an error, I would address it privately and frame the conversation around learning and improvement. "Let's talk about what happened with the client presentation and figure out how to handle similar situations better in the future." This approach was much more effective than public humiliation or harsh criticism.

I also made sure to give positive feedback regularly, not just during annual reviews. When someone did good work or handled a difficult situation well, I would acknowledge it immediately. People need to know when they're succeeding, not just when they're falling short.

Another key lesson was the importance of protecting my team from organizational dysfunction above us. I had worked for too many managers who passed down every bit of stress and chaos from their superiors. I made it a priority to shield my people from unnecessary drama and politics while keeping them informed about things that actually affected their work.

When senior management would come up with unrealistic deadlines or poorly thought-out initiatives, I would push back where possible and translate their demands into reasonable work plans for my team. This sometimes put me in conflict with my own managers, but I believed my first loyalty was to the people who worked for me.

I learned to be transparent about challenges and constraints without making my team feel helpless or demotivated. If budget cuts meant we couldn't hire additional staff, I would explain the situation honestly and work with the team to figure out how to adjust our plans. People can handle difficult news much better than they can handle being kept in the dark or lied to.

One of the hardest aspects of management was learning when and how to have difficult conversations. I had seen too many managers either avoid addressing performance problems until they became crises or handle them so poorly that they created bigger problems.

When someone on my team was struggling, I tried to address it quickly and directly. I would have a private conversation to understand what was causing the issues and work with them to develop an improvement plan. Sometimes the problems were related to unclear expectations or inadequate resources rather than individual performance.

Not every difficult conversation resulted in improvement. I had to terminate two people over the years for performance issues that couldn't be resolved. These decisions were never easy, but I learned that keeping someone who can't do the job is unfair to them, unfair to their teammates, and ultimately harmful to the organization.

The most rewarding part of management was watching people on my team grow and advance in their careers. I made it a priority to understand each person's career goals and help them develop the skills and experience they needed to achieve them.

Several people who worked for me went on to management roles themselves, and I took pride in knowing I had helped prepare them for that responsibility.

I also learned the importance of admitting when I was wrong and apologizing when I made mistakes. Too many of the toxic managers I had worked for were incapable of acknowledging their errors or taking responsibility for problems they created. I tried to model the behavior I wanted to see from others.

Looking back on my years as a manager, I made plenty of mistakes. I sometimes let problems fester too long before addressing them. I occasionally made decisions too quickly without getting enough input from my team. I didn't always communicate as clearly as I should have.

But I tried to learn from those mistakes and do better. I asked for feedback regularly and took it seriously when people told me I could improve. I read books about management and leadership, attended training sessions, and sought advice from other managers I respected.

The experience taught me that good management is a skill that can be learned and improved, just like any other professional capability. It requires self-awareness, empathy, good communication skills, and the willingness to make difficult decisions when necessary.

Most importantly, it requires remembering that your job as a manager is to help other people succeed, not to make yourself feel important or powerful. The best managers I worked for understood that their success was measured by their team's success, not by how much control they could exert or how much credit they could claim.

If you find yourself in a management role, use your experiences with bad bosses as a guide for what not to do. But don't stop there. Figure out what good leadership actually looks like and work to develop those skills. Your team deserves better than just "not awful." They deserve a manager who actively helps them succeed and creates an environment where they can do their best work.

Breaking the cycle of bad management starts with each of us who has the opportunity to lead others. Learn from the mistakes of the toxic bosses you've endured, but more importantly, learn how to do the job right.

# Chapter 18: Toxic Bosses in the Remote/Hybrid World



The shift to remote and hybrid work environments changed many things about how we work, but it didn't eliminate toxic bosses. Instead, it gave them new tools for dysfunction while making their behavior harder to document and escape. Some toxic managers actually became worse in remote environments, while others struggled to adapt their control tactics to a distributed workforce.

I experienced this firsthand when I was working for a manager named Rita during the transition to remote work. Rita had always been a micromanager, but when we went fully remote, her need to control everything became pathological. She couldn't stand not being able to physically see what everyone was doing at all times.

Within the first week of remote work, Rita instituted what she called "productivity monitoring." She required everyone on the team to install software that tracked our keystrokes, mouse movements, and took screenshots of our computers every few minutes. She claimed this was necessary to ensure we were working effectively from home.

The surveillance software was just the beginning. Rita started scheduling multiple video calls throughout the day, ostensibly for "team coordination" but really so she could check up on us. We had a mandatory 15-minute video call first thing in the morning, another at lunch, and a wrap-up call at the end of the day. She would also schedule random "quick check-ins" with individual team members.

During these video calls, Rita would scrutinize our backgrounds, comment on our appearance, and ask detailed questions about exactly what we had been working on since the last call. If someone's camera was off or they looked distracted, she would make passive-aggressive comments about "commitment to the team."

The worst part was how she used the remote environment to extend her control beyond normal business hours. Because we were all working from home, Rita felt justified in sending emails and Slack messages at all hours of the day and night. She expected immediate responses, regardless of the time.

"Just because we're working from home doesn't mean we're unavailable," she would say. "We need to be more responsive to maintain team cohesion."

Rita also weaponized the hybrid schedule against us. On days when some team members were in the office and others were remote, she would hold important meetings in person without properly including the remote participants. She would make decisions during casual hallway conversations that the remote workers weren't privy to.

When remote team members complained about being excluded, Rita would say they should come into the office more often if they wanted to stay informed. But when they did come in, she would criticize them for not being consistent with their remote schedule.

The psychological impact of Rita's remote management style was severe. The constant surveillance made everyone paranoid about taking breaks, getting coffee, or stepping away from their computers for any reason. The after-hours communication demands meant work stress followed us into our homes in ways it never had before.

Several team members started experiencing anxiety about video calls because they knew Rita would be analyzing their every expression and gesture. Others became obsessive about their home office setups, spending money they couldn't afford on better cameras and lighting because Rita had made comments about their video quality.

The isolation of remote work made Rita's abuse even more damaging. When you're being harassed by a boss in person, at least your colleagues can see what's happening. In a remote environment, much of the toxic behavior happens in private one-on-one calls or direct messages.

Rita would have individual video calls with team members where she would spend 45 minutes criticizing their work, questioning their commitment, and making veiled threats about their job security. Because these conversations happened in private, other team members had no idea how badly their colleagues were being treated.

This isolation also made it harder to build alliances with coworkers. The casual conversations that happen naturally in an office environment, where you might discover that other people are also having problems with the boss, don't happen as easily in remote settings.

Rita also discovered new ways to abuse her power through technology. She would schedule mandatory video calls during people's lunch breaks or at the end of the day when they were trying to wrap up work. She would require cameras to be on for all meetings, even when people were dealing with home distractions like children or pets.

She used the screen-sharing feature during calls to take control of people's computers and criticize their work in real-time while the rest of the team watched. This public humiliation was even more uncomfortable in a video call setting than it would have been in person.

The documentation challenges in a remote environment were significant. While some of Rita's behavior was captured in emails and Slack messages, much of it happened during video calls that weren't recorded. Her tone of voice, facial expressions, and body language conveyed hostility and contempt, but these things are harder to document than written communications.

Rita was also careful to avoid putting her most abusive behavior in writing. She would send professional-sounding emails that seemed reasonable on the surface, then follow up with hostile video calls where she would berate people for not reading between the lines or understanding her "real" expectations.

The remote environment gave Rita plausible deniability for many of her toxic behaviors. When team members complained about the excessive surveillance, she claimed it was necessary for "maintaining productivity standards" in a remote environment. When people objected to after-hours communication, she said it was required for "global collaboration" and "business continuity."

She framed her micromanagement as "supporting remote workers" and her intrusive questions as "ensuring everyone has the resources they need." She had learned to use the language of remote work best practices to justify behavior that was actually abusive.

Fighting back against toxic bosses in remote environments requires different strategies than in traditional office settings. The lack of casual interaction with colleagues means you need to be more intentional about building relationships and documenting patterns of abuse.

I started reaching out to my teammates individually to share experiences and compare notes about Rita's behavior. I discovered that everyone was dealing with similar harassment but had been suffering in isolation. Once we started talking, we were able to support each other and document the patterns more effectively.

The technology that enabled Rita's surveillance and micromanagement also provided tools for documenting her behavior. I started taking screenshots of her invasive messages and scheduling demands. I used calendar invitations and email timestamps to document the excessive meeting requirements and after-hours expectations.

I also learned to be strategic about video call recordings. While Rita didn't allow us to record team meetings, I started having one-on-one conversations with her over video while using screen recording software to capture her abusive behavior. (Recording laws vary significantly by state and country — some jurisdictions require all parties to consent. Check the laws in your location before recording any conversation.)

The remote environment also made it easier to job search discreetly. I could take phone interviews from home during lunch breaks without Rita knowing. I could research other opportunities and update my LinkedIn profile without worrying about colleagues seeing what I was doing.

Eventually, three of us left the team within a six-week period. The talent exodus finally got senior management's attention, and they started investigating Rita's management practices. The documentation we had gathered about her surveillance, harassment, and after-hours demands made it difficult for her to deny the problems.

Rita was eventually moved to a different role where she couldn't manage people directly, but not before she had driven away several talented employees and created a toxic remote work culture that took months to rebuild.

The experience taught me that remote and hybrid work environments don't eliminate toxic management behaviors. They just change how those behaviors manifest and how you need to respond to them.

Toxic managers in remote environments often become more controlling rather than less, using technology as a tool for surveillance and harassment. They may exploit the isolation of remote work to abuse people privately or use the flexibility of remote schedules to extend their control beyond normal business hours.

If you're dealing with a toxic boss in a remote or hybrid environment, document everything obsessively. Take screenshots of invasive messages, save recordings of abusive video calls when possible, and keep detailed records of unreasonable demands and expectations.

Build relationships with your colleagues intentionally, since the natural relationship-building that happens in office environments may not occur remotely. Reach out to teammates privately to compare experiences and build support networks.

Set and enforce boundaries around your availability and workspace. Just because you're working from home doesn't mean your boss has the right to invade your personal time and space. Push back against surveillance software, excessive video monitoring, and after-hours communication demands.

Remember that many of the fundamental principles for dealing with toxic bosses still apply in remote environments. Document the behavior, build your exit strategy, and don't let isolation prevent you from seeking support and taking action to protect yourself.

The remote work revolution promised to give workers more flexibility and autonomy, but toxic managers found ways to subvert those benefits. Don't let them succeed. Your home should be a refuge from workplace stress, not an extension of a toxic office environment.

# Chapter 19: The Freelancing Alternative

---

*"The secret of getting ahead is getting started." — Mark Twain*

---

After dealing with toxic bosses for decades, I eventually realized there was another option I hadn't seriously considered: working for myself. Freelancing and consulting offered a way to escape the dysfunction of corporate hierarchies entirely, though it came with its own set of challenges and risks.

My first taste of freelancing came out of necessity rather than choice. I had just quit a job working for a particularly abusive manager without having another position lined up. While I was job hunting, a former colleague reached out asking if I could help with a short-term project at his company. They needed someone with my specific technical skills for about six weeks.

"We can't hire you as an employee because of budget constraints," he explained, "but we could bring you in as a contractor. The pay would be better than your last job, and you'd have a lot more autonomy."

I was skeptical. Freelancing seemed risky and unpredictable. What about health insurance? What about steady income? What if I couldn't find enough work to pay my bills?

But I was also tired of dealing with corporate politics and dysfunctional management. The idea of working directly with clients, without layers of incompetent middle management, was appealing.

I took the contract, and it opened my eyes to possibilities I hadn't considered before.

Working as a contractor was liberating in ways I hadn't expected. When the client asked me to do something, I could focus on delivering results instead of navigating office politics.

When I had questions or concerns, I could communicate directly with the decision-makers instead of going through multiple layers of management.

Most importantly, if a client turned out to be difficult or unreasonable, I knew the engagement was temporary. I didn't have to worry about being stuck with a toxic boss for years. When the project ended, I could choose whether to work with them again.

The financial benefits were significant too. As a contractor, I was earning about 40% more per hour than I had as an employee, even after accounting for the lack of benefits. The client was getting specialized expertise for a specific project, and I was getting paid well for delivering it.

After completing that first contract successfully, I found that word-of-mouth referrals led to other opportunities. Within six months, I had more work than I could handle and was turning down projects that didn't interest me or that came from clients who seemed problematic.

The experience taught me that freelancing could provide not just an escape from bad bosses, but also a path to greater professional and financial freedom. However, it wasn't without its challenges.

The most obvious challenge is the irregular income. As an employee, you know you'll get a paycheck every two weeks regardless of how much work you actually accomplish. As a freelancer, your income depends directly on the work you complete and your ability to collect payment from clients.

This means you need to be much more disciplined about financial planning. I learned to save aggressively during busy periods to cover expenses during slower times. I also had to get comfortable with the uncertainty of not knowing exactly how much money I'd make from month to month.

Health insurance was another major consideration. As an employee, your health insurance is typically subsidized by your employer. As a freelancer, you pay the full cost yourself. This can be expensive, especially if you have a family to cover.

I solved this problem by purchasing a high-deductible health plan paired with a health savings account. The monthly premiums were manageable, and the HSA provided tax advantages while building a fund for medical expenses. It wasn't as comprehensive as the insurance I'd had as an employee, but it protected me from catastrophic costs.

The isolation was something I hadn't anticipated. Working from home or client sites meant I didn't have daily interactions with colleagues. I missed the casual conversations and collaborative problem-solving that happen naturally in office environments.

I addressed this by joining professional associations, attending industry meetups, and occasionally working from co-working spaces where I could be around other professionals. These activities also helped with networking and finding new clients.

One of the biggest challenges was learning to run a business. As a freelancer, you're not just doing the technical work you were hired for. You're also handling sales, marketing, accounting, project management, and customer service.

I had to learn how to write proposals, negotiate contracts, track expenses, send invoices, and follow up on late payments. I needed to understand tax implications, liability insurance, and legal requirements for independent contractors.

This business side of freelancing was initially overwhelming, but I found that most of the skills were learnable and that there were tools and services to help with many of the administrative tasks.

Setting boundaries became crucial in ways I hadn't experienced as an employee. Some clients assumed that because I was a contractor, I was available 24/7. Others tried to expand the scope of projects without adjusting the timeline or compensation.

I learned to be very specific about what was included in each project, what my availability would be, and how changes to scope would be handled. Having clear contracts and communication upfront prevented most problems and made it easier to address issues when they did arise.

The marketing aspect was probably the most challenging for someone with a technical background. I had to learn how to explain my value proposition to potential clients, build a professional website, maintain a LinkedIn presence, and ask satisfied clients for referrals.

I discovered that my reputation and the quality of my work were my most important marketing tools. Delivering excellent results on time and within budget led to repeat business and referrals more effectively than any advertising or networking efforts.

After several years of successful freelancing, I had built up enough savings and client relationships to feel secure about the lifestyle. The irregular income had become more predictable as I developed ongoing relationships with several clients who provided steady work.

The freedom was extraordinary. I could choose which projects to take based on interest, compensation, and the quality of the client relationship. I could set my own schedule and work from anywhere with an internet connection. I could take time off without asking permission or worrying about how it would affect my performance review.

Most importantly, I never had to deal with toxic bosses again. If a client turned out to be difficult, unreasonable, or abusive, I could complete the current project and decline future work. I had eliminated the power dynamic that makes bad employee-manager relationships so destructive.

Freelancing isn't for everyone. It requires self-discipline, business skills, financial discipline, and comfort with uncertainty. You need to be able to work independently and manage your own time effectively. You also need skills that are in demand and that clients are willing to pay well for.

But for people who are tired of corporate dysfunction and want more control over their professional lives, freelancing can be an excellent alternative. It's particularly attractive for those who have specialized expertise that's valuable to multiple organizations but don't want to be tied to any single employer.

Even if you don't want to freelance full-time, part-time consulting work can provide valuable benefits. It gives you additional income, exposes you to different industries and business models, and builds a network of professional relationships outside your current employer.

Part-time freelancing also serves as a safety net. If you lose your job or decide you need to leave a toxic situation quickly, having established client relationships makes the transition much easier.

I eventually returned to traditional employment when I found an opportunity with an exceptional manager and organization. But the years I spent freelancing taught me valuable lessons about business, gave me financial security, and proved that there are alternatives to the traditional corporate career path.

The experience also made me a better employee. Having run my own business made me more aware of costs, deadlines, and client needs. I understood the pressure that managers face and was more effective at communicating the value of my work.

Most importantly, knowing that I could successfully work for myself eliminated the fear that kept me trapped in toxic employment situations. I never again felt like I had to tolerate abuse or dysfunction just to keep a paycheck coming.

If you're dealing with a toxic boss and feeling trapped by financial obligations, consider whether freelancing might be a viable option for your situation. Start by taking on small projects in your spare time to test the waters and build up your skills and client base.

You might discover, as I did, that working for yourself provides not just an escape from bad bosses, but a path to greater professional fulfillment and financial freedom.

# Conclusion

As I'm sure you've realized from reading this book, there are many terrible bosses out there. But keep in mind that your boss is a human being just like you, and they will have good days and bad days. Just because your supervisor has a bad day doesn't mean they're toxic. It just means the day didn't go well, and they got a little emotional.

This kind of thing is a normal part of working with people. Sometimes people lie, and that doesn't mean they are pathological liars. Occasionally, a boss will get angry and might even yell, but that doesn't mean they're abusive. Every once in a while, a boss will do something that's questionable ethically, but that doesn't mean they are fundamentally corrupt.

Take things in context and don't overreact to minor personality quirks and changes. Act like an adult, and allow the other adults around you to have their occasional off moments.

On the other hand, if the boss is continually harassing you, is making your workplace hostile, has questionable sanity, or is asking you to compromise your integrity, then you need to take action. Just make sure your personal life and finances are in good shape, so you have options.

After thirty-three years in corporate America, I've learned that the patterns repeat everywhere. The racist who nearly said the n-word in front of witnesses. The religious bigot who demanded I hide my faith. The pathological liar who stole my commission. The micromanager who timed bathroom breaks. The psychotic executive who needed armed security to be fired. The sexual predator who used power to hunt subordinates.

These aren't isolated incidents. They're character types that exist in organizations everywhere, and they often get promoted precisely because their dysfunction looks like strength to people who don't understand the difference.

I've also learned that the systems supposedly designed to protect employees are largely useless. HR departments exist to protect companies from lawsuits, not employees from bad managers. The "investigation" process is often just theater designed to document reasons why the complainer should be fired. Policies and procedures mean nothing when toxic managers decide they don't apply to them.

Take back control of your professional life. You don't have to tolerate abuse, harassment, discrimination, or unethical demands from anyone, regardless of their title. You have options, even when it doesn't feel like it.

The key is preparation. Build your escape fund. Keep your skills current and marketable. Document everything. Maintain your professional network. Never let yourself become so dependent on one job that you can't afford to leave a toxic situation.

Good managers like Steve Davis and John Shields exist. They're rare, but they're out there. They understand that their job is to remove obstacles, not create them. They communicate clearly, delegate appropriately, treat people with respect, and make decisions based on what's best for the work and the people doing it.

When you find managers like this, learn from them. When you become a manager yourself, remember what good leadership looks like and what damage bad leadership causes.

The workplace doesn't have to be a source of trauma and misery. Yes, there will always be difficult people and challenging situations. But the level of dysfunction I've described in this book isn't normal, and it isn't something you have to accept.

Your integrity is more important than any job. Your mental and physical health matter more than any paycheck. Your self-respect is worth more than job security with a toxic boss.

I wrote this book for everyone who's ever wondered if they were losing their mind because their boss's behavior was so irrational. For everyone who's been afraid to speak up because they needed the job. For everyone who's sat in their car after work, too beaten down to drive home.

You're not alone. You're not crazy. And you don't have to stay trapped.

These are the lessons I learned the hard way over thirty-three years. The racist managers who made work hell for good people. The liars who stole commissions and broke promises. The micromanagers who destroyed productivity through control addiction. The psychotics who created genuine safety concerns. The predators who used power to abuse subordinates.

I survived all of them, and so can you. But you don't have to just survive. You can build the skills, financial security, and professional relationships that give you real choices about where and how you work.

Don't waste years hoping that toxic managers will change or that broken systems will protect you. Take control of your own career. Build your escape fund. Document the bad behavior. Develop marketable skills. And when you encounter truly toxic leadership, have the courage to leave.

Life is too short to spend your working hours being abused by people who should be providing leadership and support. There are better jobs and better managers out there. But you'll never find them if you're too damaged or too trapped to pursue them.

The patterns I've described in this book repeat because good people stay silent and tolerate bad behavior for too long. Change starts with people who decide they've had enough and are willing to take action to protect themselves and others.

Your career is your responsibility. Your wellbeing is your responsibility. Don't delegate either to managers who have demonstrated they can't be trusted with them.

You deserve better than what too many of these managers offer. With preparation, documentation, and the courage to act when necessary, you can get it.

# About the Author

Richard Lowe survived thirty-three years in corporate America, working his way through technology companies, startups, and retail organizations. During that time, he encountered every type of toxic manager described in this book–and learned hard lessons about protecting himself from workplace dysfunction.

After experiencing racist bosses, pathological liars, micromanagers, and genuinely unstable executives, Lowe developed the documentation strategies, exit planning techniques, and mental health preservation methods outlined in these pages. His approach combines practical workplace survival tactics with the financial and career planning necessary to escape toxic situations.

When not writing about workplace survival, Lowe has authored over sixty books on topics ranging from technology to historical memoirs. His diverse background gives him perspective on how toxic management patterns repeat across industries and organizational levels.

Lowe believes no one should have to tolerate abuse, harassment, or unethical behavior from anyone, regardless of their title. This book provides the tools to recognize toxic situations, protect yourself legally and financially, and build the career independence that gives you real choices about where and how you work.

# Books by Richard Lowe

See books by Richard Lowe at

https://masterofworlds.com


Get free publishing insights and industry updates at

https://thewritingking.substack.com


For ghostwriting and book coaching services see

https://thewritingking.com